"Pastor Lawrence Khong is a cutting-edge Christian leader who has established a model church for the 21st century. This book contains the amazing story behind this church's phenomenal growth, along with excellent principles for all churches everywhere. Highly recommended inspirational reading!"

Mark Conner
Senior Minister, Waverley Christian Fellowship, Melbourne, Australia

"This is an excellent book for traditional churches that are in the process of transitioning into a cell church. It contains not only the theology of the cell system but also the principles that can be applied to any church. The book is born out of Rev. Khong's past experiences and his church's struggles over its transition."

Yoshito Ishihara
Senior Pastor, International Christian Baptist Church, Gamagori, Japan
(Coordinator of Japan Cell Church Mission Network)

"This book will be like a light from heaven for many people who feel that church ought to be better than they are experiencing. It is an honest account of God's vision becoming a reality in the life of a pastor, a church, and a world movement. Every church leader and every member should read it. It will rattle the windows and open the doors."

Dr. Lorna Jenkins
Timothy Ministries, Auckland, New Zealand

"Lawrence Khong writes the way he preaches—with a compelling passion and enthusiasm that is captivating, mingled with sound and solid biblical and practical truths. For the past decade I have been very closely associated with Lawrence and Faith Community Baptist Church, and I have sat under these teachings on many occasions. I know it works! I have applied them in my own church and ministry with much success and now I am teaching them to leaders in other countries. Few people have impacted my life like Lawrence Khong. I am sure his book will touch your life and ministry in a powerful way and propel you toward your destiny of touching lives for the kingdom of God!"

Dr. Charles C. Carroll
Senior Pastor, Community of Praise Baptist Church, Singapore

"As a pioneer and practitioner in the cell church movement, Pastor Lawrence Khong is most qualified to address this subject. The cell church holds promise to be *the* new wineskin at the local church level to bring in the end-time harvest.

His willingness to share his heart with thousands of leaders in Africa is bearing much fruit in the continent today. I believe this very practical book will help those of us in the Apostolic movement to spread the word on the cell church faster than ever before.

I can highly recommend this as a handbook to help you either transition your church or establish a cell church in your part of the world."

Willie Crew

World Mission Center, Pretoria, South Africa

"I greatly admire Pastor Khong's understanding of the cell church and I particularly like the word "Apostolic" in the title, which richly expresses the mission-minded, pioneering, challenging, proactive, strategic, structural, and anointed nature of the cell church. This book embraces the core substance of Rev. Khong's pastoral experiences, and contains the blueprints and methodology that God has given to the church in our generation. More importantly, it prepares the church for revival and is a path to fulfilling the Great Commission." (ORIGINALLY IN CHINESE)

Abraham Ku

Senior Pastor, New Life Cell Church, Taipei, Taiwan

"Rev. Lawrence Khong has been ministering to churches all over the world for many years. But the greatest burden upon his heart is to win cities and nations for Christ through the cell church. For the past three to four years, Rev. Khong and his team from Faith Community Baptist Church have committed themselves to training pastors from transitioning cell churches in Taiwan. Many Taiwanese pastors have benefited from such a training and churches have grown significantly as a result. Of these, Taipei Ling-Leung Church has benefited the most. It has also experienced the greatest change. This book culls the essence of Rev. Khong's past experiences—his own experiences into the cell church as well as his apostolic ministry to transitioning cell churches all over the world. May God use this book to bless many churches and co-workers in Jesus Christ." (ORIGINALLY IN CHINESE)

Chow Shen Chu

Senior Pastor, Taipei Ling-Leung Church, Taipei, Taiwan

"After having read this book, I am deeply moved and filled with great admiration! *The Apostolic Cell Church* covers the plenary topics presented by Rev. Lawrence Khong during the annual International Conference on Cell Group Churches. In this book, Rev. Khong also shares his own experiences and struggles with great transparency. I suggest that every member of the cell church get hold of this book because it will surely inspire you to be a 'spiritual eagle' in your daily living and in your ministry, helping you to soar in the highest glory of God." (ORIGINALLY IN CHINESE)

Peter Chu
Senior Pastor, Taipei Truth Church, Taipei, Taiwan

"Around the world, God has raised many individuals who are modern-day prophets to our time and to the church. Individuals who challenge us to think differently. Lawrence Khong is one of those individuals. Not only has he challenged us to think differently, he has gone out and put his ideas into practice and built a thriving and dynamic church which is based on cell principles. This cell church is an encouragement and a challenge to us all.

In Lawrence's book, he outlines the key dynamics that have enabled him to build this church, laying out what God has said to him and the principles behind cell church. I think this book will be an encouragement for all of us who are looking at church in this new millennium and wondering what it should be like. We need to listen clearly, we need to listen carefully and prayerfully to the challenges that Lawrence puts before us."

Laurence Singlehurst
YWAM England, Director, Herts, England, UK

"*The Apostolic Cell Church* by Lawrence Kong demands our attention since it comes from a man who has experienced spiritual success in being and doing what he is writing about. This book is a must for churches who wish to change and so impact the world in a new way to complete world mission."

Roger T. Forster
Icthus Christian Fellowship, London, England, UK

"Lawrence Khong is a reformer for this hour of the church. God has revealed to him strategies to see that every believer is fully functioning. The cell church strategy is one of God's major plans to see the church rise up in power in this new millennium."

Dr. Cindy Jacobs
Co-Founder, Generals of Intercession, Colorado Springs, Colorado, USA

"There are many books on cell churches written for the pastor or leader, but there are few writers who have modeled the cell church concept. Lawrence Khong has 'gone over Jordan' before us; he has spied out the land and has come back with a great report. We can build Apostolic Cell Churches for the 21st century. This book is more than instruction; it is impartation. It is a map laid out by one who has made the journey. Thank you, Lawrence, for your investment into this generation of pastors and leaders."

Frank Damazio
Senior Pastor, City Bible Church, Portland, Oregon, USA

"Everyone is searching for meaning in life. If a man can fulfill God's call in his life, then he would have lived a worthwhile life. *The Apostolic Cell Church* is a living example that shows us that every Christian can live out God's purposes for his life, and soar on wings of eagle for the glory of God. If you are a Christian or leader in your church, you must read this book." (ORIGINALLY IN CHINESE)

Joseph Tsai
Senior Pastor, Home of Christians, Eastern Los Angeles, California, USA

"This book describes how Rev. Lawrence Khong received from God a revelation about the apostolic cell church. In 1998, Rev. Khong shared this revelation with the delegates at a cell conference during the Thanksgiving week in Chicago, and this brought about a great awakening. I truly believe that this revelation is biblical and is an instrument that heralds breakthroughs in our churches today—breakthroughs in terms of growth in quantity and quality. It also mobilizes the church to fulfill the Great Commission by the taking of active steps to evangelize and reach out to lost souls." (ORIGINALLY IN CHINESE)

Joseph Y.S. Tai
Senior Pastor, Christian Assembly of Suburban Chicago, Illinois, USA

"This book dynamically illustrates God's call and anointing upon Rev. Lawrence Khong's life and reveals God's strategy for reviving the church before the second coming of Christ. The United Christian Church in California, USA, was greatly attracted by the vision and strategy of the cell church in 1996. When we started applying these cell church concepts and principles into our church, we experienced the outworking of these principles in very real terms. I believe *The Apostolic Cell Church* has eternal value in the Kingdom of God and will benefit many struggling churches." (ORIGINALLY IN CHINESE)

Philip Chen
Senior Pastor, The United Christian Church, California, USA

THE
APOSTOLIC
CELL
CHURCH

PRACTICAL STRATEGIES
FOR GROWTH AND OUTREACH

FROM THE STORY OF
FAITH COMMUNITY BAPTIST CHURCH

Lawrence Khong

THE APOSTOLIC CELL CHURCH
Practical Strategies for Growth and Outreach
from the story of
Faith Community Baptist Church

COPYRIGHT © 2000 LAWRENCE KHONG

Published by **TOUCH Ministries International Pte Ltd**
66 East Coast Road #06-00
Singapore 428778
Tel: 65-440-8821 Fax: 65-345-6415
E-mail: tmi_publications@touch.org.sg
Website: www.tmi.com.sg

ISBN 981-04-1259-2

International Distribution:

TOUCH Resource Pte Ltd
Blk 203B Henderson Road
#04-06 Singapore 159548
Tel: 65-377-3286, Fax: 65-377-3285
E-mail: touchres@pacific.net.sg

FCBC International
Mailing Address:
P. O. Box 911 Denton, Texas 76202-0911, USA
Tel: 1-940-382-3035, 1-888-404-3222 (toll-free)
Fax: 1-940-484-6097
E-mail: publications@wci.org
Website: www.fcbccells.org

Please contact us for more information on other cell church materials.
Printed in the Republic of Singapore

A TMI PUBLICATION
FOR THE CELL CHURCH

~ Contents ~

~ FOREWORD ~

The title of the book you have in your hands is very significant. Don't let the meaning of the word "apostolic" escape you. During the decade of the 1990s, many books on the cell church were published. But none of them were books on *The Apostolic Cell Church*.

David Yonggi Cho, pastor of Yoido Full Gospel Church of Seoul, Korea, was the most visible pioneer of the cell church movement. He will be honored for this highly important contribution when books on recent church history are written. But Cho was a pioneer of the first generation of cell churches. Now that we are in the 21st Century, we are also entering a new generation of cell churches. The best I can see the movement of history in the making, the baton for leadership of the cell church movement is passing from David Yonggi Cho to Lawrence Khong, the author of this book.

One of the reasons that God has assigned this new role to Lawrence Khong is that Lawrence not only is an apostle, but he also understands the gift and office of apostle, he practices it in his ministry, and he knows how to communicate the ramifications to others. Dr. Cho certainly is an apostle as well and he has modeled apostolic leadership for decades, but his generation did not use the title nor did they have the paradigm to articulate how the ministry of apostle operates in the body of Christ. That paradigm only began to develop in the 1990s, and it is still new, and in fact suspect, to many Christian leaders. Not to Lawrence Khong, however. He is among the pioneers who recognize that apostles and prophets are truly the foundation of the church (see Ephesians 2:20), and he has accepted public ordination as an apostle.

How does this apply to cell churches? In the past, many have operated on the principle that cell groups help churches grow because

8

of the way they change the structure and the operation of the local church. This is correct, but it is only one variable. It does not explain why some local churches have bought into the cell principle heavily, have changed the structure of their church, but their church hasn't grown. The explanation of this, as I see it, is another equally important variable, namely church leadership.

It is in this area of leadership that Lawrence Khong's book on the cell church stands out over the others. This is a book on cell group ministry, but much more. The philosophy of ministry of Faith Community Baptist Church is spelled out in detail, and it is the interfacing of the different elements in this philosophy of ministry that have contributed to making FCBC one of the highest profile cell-based megachurches in the world today.

The Apostolic Cell Church is the textbook for this second generation of cell churches. It will provide you the keys you need to unlock the barriers to growth in your church and to see your church become everything that God wants it to be!

Dr. C. Peter Wagner
Chancellor
Wagner Leadership Institute
Colorado Springs, Colorado, USA

— PREFACE —

Friend, we are living in the most exciting days of planet earth! A new wave of the Holy Spirit is sweeping the world as never before in history.

As we enter the third millennium since our Lord walked among us, fresh outpourings of the Spirit are bringing renewal, revival, awakening, and even transformation to cities across the globe. This "new wine" carries a special anointing to flow out to previously untouched segments of society with the gospel of Jesus Christ. The kingdom of God continues to advance at unprecedented rates as eager seekers quench their spiritual thirst in the life-giving stream.

New wine can be exciting, even intoxicating. But it also presents special challenges to those who receive it. Consider the words of Jesus in Luke 5:37-38: "And no one pours new wine into old wineskins. If he does, the new wine will burst the skins, the wine will run out and the wineskins will be ruined. No, new wine must be poured into new wineskins."

As I look at the body of Christ throughout the world today, I see God preparing fresh wineskins. Rigid and inflexible church structures cannot easily expand to receive the fruit of this new spiritual outpouring. We need forms that can stretch and grow, making room quickly and easily for many more people to join the community of believers.

Wolfgang Simson, strategist with the Dawn International Network, writes in the August 1999 issue of the *DAWN Report:*

> In rediscovering the gospel of salvation by faith and
> grace alone, [Martin] Luther started to reform the Church

through a *reformation of theology*. In the 18th century through movements like the Moravians there was a recovery of a new intimacy with God, which led to the Second Reformation, a *reformation of spirituality*. Now God is touching the wineskins themselves, initiating a Third Reformation, a *reformation of structure*. (p. 6, emphasis original)

One of the major new structures God is raising up in our days is the cell church. As Wolfgang Simson implies by using the word "reformation," the concept behind the cell church actually goes back to the New Testament. In the first century, small groups of believers "broke bread in their homes and ate together with glad and sincere hearts, praising God and enjoying the favor of all the people. And the Lord added to their number daily those who were being saved" (Acts 2:46–47). These home fellowship groups provided a place for praise and worship of God, nurture and discipleship of believers, and incorporation of unbelievers. The modern cell group follows a similar pattern.

Just as our biological bodies are made up of cells, so the cell group serves as the building block of the cell church. It is living and dynamic. It grows and multiplies. The cell pulses with the life of the church, from the power of the Holy Spirit flowing through it.

Because the cell's built-in genetic code propels it toward growth, I believe the cell church is far and away the best model for expanding a body of believers through outreach. By this I mean that the cell church does not simply attract existing Christians who add to its numbers by transfer growth. The cell church provides a thriving structure that effectively reaches and draws in the lost and unchurched of our communities. Unless we build channels and avenues to the unsaved, most of the people in our cities, our nations, and our world will remain parched and unnourished by the spring of Christ's living water.

Most of the world's largest congregations are cell churches. They not only win the lost in greater numbers than the average church; they also retain more new converts, because the cell design offers a natural environment where young believers can readily be enfolded, equipped, and released into ministry.

Cell churches come in various styles. Our experience at Faith Community Baptist Church in Singapore provides just one model of a growing cell church. Whether following FCBC-style or some other style, a congregation that has committed to the vision and principles of the cell church will experience the heartbeat of God for His beloved lost sheep.

In our days the Lord is also renewing and reinstating the role of the apostle in the body of Christ. Both the spiritual gift and the office of apostle have received growing recognition and affirmation in contemporary Christianity. When Ephesians 4:11 says "It was he who gave some to be apostles..." I do not believe God meant this gift as a temporary blessing for one short season of Christian history. The word "apostle" in Greek indicates one who is sent out with a commission. The apostles of the first century were given anointing and authority to take the gospel to the ends of the earth. Since the Great Commission still awaits completion today, contemporary apostles have a crucial role in leading and mobilizing God's people to extend His kingdom into new territories.

Within the cell church movement, God is appointing apostolic leaders. These anointed leaders have received God's commission to pioneer and unite cell churches in local, regional, and global networks. Such networks encourage and empower the churches as they reach out to establish vibrant, witnessing communities among those who have yet to hear the Good News.

Embracing the apostolic cell church requires a paradigm shift for those who have known only traditional models of church structure. It is easier to start and grow a cell church from scratch than to reconstruct a traditional, program-based church to align with cell church principles and practice. Transitioning an existing church always presents challenges and difficulties. But, I assure you, it is worth it. The cell church offers the best strategy I know to fulfill the vision of equipping Christ's body for ongoing growth and outreach to the lost.

Matthew 24:14 tells us that the triumphal return of Jesus Christ depends on the spread of the gospel message to all peoples everywhere. When this realization has captured our hearts, we will be motivated to do everything we can to bring about that goal. The wineskins of our churches should stand ready to grow and expand as we pray for and receive the immense outpouring of the Holy Spirit in these last days. And when increasing numbers of individuals become saved and changed by God's power, the whole community begins to experience transformation. The kingdom of God comes, and the glory of the King rises among us.

If this is your dream, read on to see how the cell church can help make it come true.

— Acknowledgement —

The ability to edit well is a work of art and requires a feat of skill. I therefore want to commend Jane Rumph for her dexterity in organizing materials from my manuscript and from transcripts of my sermon and teaching tapes. Her mastery of the English language and professionalism have added value to this book.

Thank you, Jane, for skillfully editing the contents in this book, and for ironing out some kinks along the way.

~ INTRODUCTION ~
by Dr. Ralph W. Neighbour, Jr.

It is with joy that I commend this recounting of the journey of Faith Community Baptist Church to you. In His plan for my life, in 1990, our Father sent me to tutor Lawrence Khong and his faithful team of cell-based believers. The five years I spent serving on his staff in Singapore are unforgettable.

Page by page, I have smiled as I read terms and concepts the Lord gave to me years ago, transferred by mentoring and then fleshed out by Pastor Khong to fit the unique culture of a city-state. In our staff planning times, his determination not to solve cell church problems by reverting to traditional methods was an awesome thing to observe. His transparency in sharing his successes and failures in this book reveals the characteristics that make him an effective cell church pastor.

The concept of "TOUCH," which stands for "Transforming Others Under Christ's Hand," was born in 1969 for the witness of my cell church in Houston, Texas, and has now been widely used around the world. The special application of "TOUCH" as presented in this book is unique to Faith Community Baptist Church. Others have adjusted the word to witness in their cultures. I celebrate its use as a Kingdom term.

Let us pray that God will raise up many more apostles like Lawrence Khong who will pioneer among us—the "sent ones" assigned not to build castles but to build Basic Christian Communities.

Dr. Ralph W. Neighbour, Jr.
Founder
TOUCH Outreach Ministries
Houston, Texas, USA

One

RISING AS AN EAGLE:

— My Personal Journey —

The 1984 Olympic games went down in history as one of the most memorable spectacles of the modern age. Moreover, outstanding athletic performances played a mere supporting role. What marked the event in Los Angeles was the manifest influence of Hollywood—the show capital of the world! The opening and closing ceremonies went over the top as eye-popping extravaganzas, each with a cast of thousands. Organizers spared no expense in pulling the heartstrings of millions of spectators around the world.

At that time I was on a missions trip in Sarawak, East Malaysia. One morning, after an extended time with the Lord in prayer, I read a fascinating report in *Time* magazine (August 6, 1984) about the opening ceremony of the Los Angeles Olympics. Part of the article described some behind-the-scenes challenges faced in putting the show together.

Plans for the opening ceremony included training a bald eagle, the national bird of the United States, to take part in the performance. The eagle would rise from the western rim of the Coliseum, soar down to the field as the national anthem played, and land on a perch designed in the form of five interlocking rings, one of the Olympic symbols.

What a great idea! What a great experience for that eagle! Imagine the privilege of performing before millions of pairs of eyes watching both in the stadium as well as around the world via television. There was, however, one problem. Finding an American bald eagle in captivity proved difficult. The bird available, named Bomber, came from the Patuxent Wildlife Research Center in Laurel, Maryland, where it had lived an almost flightless existence for 22 years. According to Steve Hoddy, the professional bird trainer tapped for the job, "it looked like a little butterball turkey." Hoddy put Bomber on a diet. He spent his days and nights with Bomber, gaining the eagle's respect, even sleeping in an easy chair with the bird on his arm. With painstaking patience and meat reward incentives, Hoddy taught Bomber to fly.

The time came for Bomber to come to the Coliseum for some dry runs. The eagle practiced its routine, took a couple of crash landings, but seemed game to carry on.

Then tragedy struck. Bomber died—reportedly from stress. The *Time* article observed: "The bird had been fat, coddled for years, and when called upon to behave like an eagle, failed."

What a sad commentary on the life of this eagle! Here was the chance of a lifetime to play an important role in the ceremony. It needed only to do what it was made for—to fly. The eagle, however, could not carry out its noble purpose.

As I read these words, the conviction of the Holy Spirit came upon me strongly. The Lord opened my eyes to see that many Christians and many churches are in the same sad state of affairs. We as His people are created to be spiritual eagles, soaring into the heights of God's glory in both life and ministry. Yet, like Bomber, we have grown fat from years of coddling. The Lord said to me, "The day is coming when many believers will be called upon to fly like spiritual eagles. On that day, many of them will fail!"

I cried to the Lord as I slipped onto my knees beside the hotel bed. "Lord, make me a spiritual eagle that will fly for you. Help me to shape a community of spiritual eagles who dare to soar to the heights of your glory, fulfilling your highest purposes for the work of your kingdom. When my church is called upon to fly for the glory of God, may we not fail!"

The Shaping of an Apostolic Community

Two years later, on August 17, 1986, I stood on the platform in a rented auditorium in Singapore to preach in the first worship service of a brand-new congregation. As I approached the pulpit, the Holy Spirit spoke clearly to my heart: "Son, today the new baby is born!" Then the words of Haggai 2:9 flooded into my mind: "'The glory of this present house will be greater than the glory of the former house...And in this place I will grant peace,' declares the LORD Almighty."

I was too emotionally worn out to be excited about the "greater glory." I simply took comfort in the fact that in this new church there would be *peace*. I had just emerged from more than a year of leadership struggle in my former church. I had grown up in that church—a Bible-believing congregation that had been growing consistently. It had been my spiritual home throughout my teenage years. The leadership of the church had clearly and lovingly affirmed my calling into the ministry. They sent me to pursue my theological training in the United States. I returned to be the pastor of the church. Within five years, it grew from 300 to 1,600 under my leadership.

During the fifth year of my pastorate, I had an unexpected encounter with the Holy Spirit that opened my heart to the reality of God's power. In that encounter, I began speaking in a new tongue. It was something I had told my congregation would not and should not ever happen in this day and age. I clearly taught them that this particular gift, together with other power gifts of the Holy Spirit, had ceased at the end of the apostolic age. I taught them so well, in fact, that the leadership of the church rejected the validity of my experience and its theological implications immediately. I realized they were doing the very thing I would have done if I were in their shoes.

I was confused. My experience completely devastated my neat and tidy theology. I could not at that point give a clear biblical understanding about what had happened. On the other hand, I could not deny the reality of that experience without compromising the witness of the Holy Spirit in my heart. Meanwhile, my ministry began falling apart. Before long, theological differences within the leadership degenerated to attacks on my personal integrity. After many months of painful struggles, I was finally asked to relinquish my role as the senior pastor of the church.

In the midst of this agonizing process, the Lord gave me a clear word from Scripture: "A woman giving birth to a child has pain because her time has come; but when her baby is born she forgets the anguish because of her joy that a child is born into the world" (John 16:21).

The Lord told me He was bringing forth a "new baby" in my life that would launch me into a new ministry. The painful struggles I was going through were the labor pains needed to deliver the child.

THE NEW BABY IS BORN

When the Lord said, "Son, today the new baby is born!" on August 17, 1986, Faith Community Baptist Church (FCBC) began. It brought unspeakable joy to my spirit. Since then, the promise of God has proved true. The glory of this ministry has far exceeded what I could have asked or thought. Indeed, in the years since then, our church has had peace.

As I am writing this, the baby has grown considerably. The attendance in our weekly worship services is pressing toward the 10,000 mark. In the past ten years, we have baptized more than 6,400 new believers. During the same period, some 17,000 persons have made professions of faith for the first time. Most significant to me is that almost every person who worships with us is also part of a cell group ministry during the week. In these small groups, we train every member to be a minister of the gospel, calling forth a higher-than-average level of commitment.

A recent survey of our congregational stewardship revealed that the giving averages more than 25 percent of the total income of all our members. This explains our annual budget of US$12 million—20 percent of which goes to world missions and another 10 percent to community services. In addition, the church owns two auditoriums costing a total of US$19 million, fully paid!

God is shaping us into an apostolic community making a global impact as a cell group church committed to world evangelization.

LESSONS FROM JOSHUA 5

Faith Community Baptist Church emerged out of the painful experience of a church split. It was one of the most difficult times of my life, but it proved absolutely necessary. The apostolic community begins with the inner life of its leader. Out of my deep brokenness before the Lord, He ingrained in me some vital spiritual lessons. In the midst of struggles, God used the fifth chapter of the book of Joshua powerfully in my life. The truths in that chapter have gripped my life and ministry ever since, and have become the foundations of the church.

Joshua 5 is an amazing chapter. The people of God had crossed the Jordan River in a miraculous display of God's power. The water stopped flowing so they could walk across on dry ground! Joshua 5:1 tells us that the kings of the land completely lost their courage to face the Israelites.

Yet the Jewish people now found themselves in a vulnerable position. They stood on the plain of the Jordan, sandwiched between the river—now flowing again—and the city of Jericho, the most formidable fortress of the land.

If I had been Joshua, I would have known exactly what to do.

"There is no time to waste. The plain is no place to dig in for a defense. Let's regroup the people. We'll set some troops to guard the women and the children, then take the rest of the young men and move on to attack Jericho. After all, the kings are frightened. Let's take advantage of their fear. This is the best time to strike the enemy. Let's charge!"

The Lord had a different idea. In verse 2 He told Joshua, "Circumcise the Israelites." This is at best surprising. In fact, it borders on the ridiculous. If I had been Joshua, I would have argued with God: "Lord, this just can't be! Don't you know how dangerous this is? Circumcision will immobilize our men for almost a week. That's exactly how the Shechemites got wiped out by the sons of Jacob" (see Genesis 34).

Circumcision was not God's only surprising directive. Later in Joshua 5, the Lord told Joshua to observe the Passover with the Israelites. This strikes me as rather premature. The Passover feast is a celebration of deliverance. I would have reasoned with God: "Lord, don't you think celebrating the Passover now seems a little presumptuous?"

VICTORY BEFORE THE BATTLE

As I meditated upon this chapter in the midst of the struggles of my ministry, the Lord surprised me with the importance of Joshua chapter five. He showed me that Joshua 5 is the most important chapter of the whole book. The passage could be appropriately entitled, "Victory Before the Battle." Here the Israelites clinched the true victory for the rest of the conquest of the land of Canaan. The military exploits of the rest of the book resulted from the victory the people received before the Lord in Joshua 5! In this chapter, the Israelites won the battle in their own lives. The rest of the story merely recounts the ingathering of the spoils of that victory.

In Joshua 5, the Lord taught the Israelites three important truths that allowed them to become the generation that inherited the promise of the land. In the same way, the Lord imbedded these three lessons into my own life so He could use me to build an apostolic community that would rise as a Joshua generation in realizing all the promises of God.

These three lessons take the form of three questions. If we answer them in accordance with God's heart, we will experience God's victory in our lives and ministry.

WHO AM I *NOT?*—CIRCUMCISE YOUR HEART

The first question is "Who am I *not?*" The first step to victory requires painful circumcision of the heart. There is no short cut. Everything displeasing to the Lord must be brutally severed. God did that in my life as part of the labor pain needed to birth a new work.

God circumcised my heart of spiritual pride and selfish ambitions. As a Southern Baptist pastor, I had the denomination's most successful ministry in the city of Singapore. As the graduate of a conservative evangelical seminary, I believed that the supernatural gifts of the Spirit had ceased. Then my experience with the Holy Spirit, accompanied by the speaking in tongues, totally messed up my tidy theology.

As God was rearranging my spiritual worldview, He was at the same time shaking up my pride. The leaders in the church pressed me for a theological basis for my experience. I was unable to reconstruct my shattered theology on the Holy Spirit. My previous attacks on charismatics had alienated me from them, so I had no one to turn to. I lost confidence even in my ability to exegete the Word of God. My experience with the Lord could not be denied. Yet I was not able to reframe my theological understanding fast enough to silence the confrontation of my church leaders.

The leaders who once held me in high regard turned against me. My world caved in. Finally, the people with whom I grew up in the church fired me. What devastation—this was the only church I had attended all my life. My tireless work led it to grow by more than 500 percent in the previous five years. Now everything fell apart. I began to see the emptiness of pursuing success in the ministry. It all felt meaningless. The Lord began to weed out from me the selfish ambition of trying to grow a big church. He taught me to seek His face. I learned to love Him and not the ministry, to fear Him and not people.

The Lord also performed major circumcision in the area of anger and bitterness. For two years, I felt a sharp cutting pain in my chest every time I thought about being fired. The pain was so real that I thought I was having a heart problem. Actually, the anger and bitterness I harbored was attacking me. In January 1988, the Lord spoke to me about going back to my former church to ask their forgiveness. When I humbled myself to do so, the Lord delivered me of the pain. After that, Faith Community Baptist Church began to grow rapidly.

When the Israelites circumcised themselves, they gained the victory. This is why the Lord said in Joshua 5:9, "Today I have rolled away the reproach of Egypt from you." In the same way, as I allowed the Lord to circumcise my heart, I saw the blessings of God in the ministry of FCBC. This is the pattern of how God has dealt with us in the years since then. Repentance always brings a new release of God's power in the church.

WHO AM I?—CELEBRATE HIS VICTORY

The second question God raises in my heart from Joshua 5 is "Who am I?" The Lord wants us not only to circumcise our hearts, but also to celebrate our victory in the Lord—the victory He has won.

This is the message of the Passover. Passover gave a clear reminder to the Jewish people that they were a redeemed people. The Israelites were to celebrate the victory of the Lord before they embarked upon the first battle. They needed to move out from a position of triumph, knowing how special they were.

Today, with Christ as our Passover Lamb, we too know how special we are to God. When we celebrate our victory in the Lord, we come to realize who we are in Him. We find our significance not in the outward results of our ministry but in the inward security of our spiritual status in Christ.

Only then can we be set free from the performance trap of ministry. Too often we tend to determine our self-worth on the basis of our success. As a consequence, we feel compelled to prove ourselves, thus reducing our efforts in the ministry to a work of the flesh. God cannot bless such endeavors. Otherwise, we would find ourselves either consumed by arrogance or crushed by the weight of responsibilities.

In the heat of the conflict in my ministry, the Lord assured me of my significance in Him. This significance is found in His great love for me. One evening, I was reading the Bible to my daughters. Priscilla was then six years old and Michelle five. We read the first chapter of Mark concerning what took place at the baptism of Jesus—how heaven opened and the Spirit descended upon Jesus as a dove. Then came the pronouncement of the Father saying, "Thou art my beloved Son, in whom I am well pleased" (Mark 1:11, KJV).

For years I had read this heavenly declaration and not understood its significance. It was to me nothing more than a divine liturgy. That evening, this statement came alive to my daughters and me. The New International Version (NIV) children's edition of the Bible, from which we were reading, gave the pronouncement this way: "You are My Son. I love you. I am pleased with you."

The simplicity of those words made the statement come alive for us. Suddenly the presence of God's love filled the room. I looked at my daughters and saw tears rolling down their cheeks. I was moved to tears as well. We began to understand what took place at the baptism of Jesus. There, God the Father leaned over the balcony of heaven to assure His Son of His love before Christ embarked upon His ministry. That evening, in my daughters' bedroom, God did the same for us. He leaned down and whispered into our ears, "You are my son, my daughter. I love you. I am pleased with you."

I had never heard my parents say those words to me. Asian culture frowns on such affirmations for fear that children will get swelled heads. We grow up knowing what we have done wrong and never what we are doing right. Then when everything was falling apart in my life, the Lord embraced me with His love. He assured me of His loving favor and how pleased He was with me.

Dignity Found in God's Approval

I began to understand that my true dignity is found not in the acceptance of others, but in the approval of my Heavenly Father. I understood why Jesus, on a human level, never betrayed the Father in the 40 days of temptation following His baptism. In the most difficult moments of His suffering, Jesus never denied His Heavenly Father. I believe Jesus gained this victory because He always remembered the words of His Father: "You are my Son. I love you. I am pleased with you."

The greatest title anyone can have is not "Reverend" or "Doctor." The greatest title is simply "child of God." No wonder the "Spirit himself testifies with our spirit that we are God's children" (Romans 8:16). When we understand how special we are as God's children, we cease from striving to prove ourselves in ministry. God then has freedom to bless the work of our hands. This is why Paul says in Romans 8:19, "The creation waits in eager expectation for the sons of God to be revealed." When we celebrate His victory in our lives, we know who we are in Him. We serve Him with great dignity and we experience the power of God in our ministry. The apostolic community is one in which every person moves out to serve with the dignity that comes from being children of the Highest God!

When the Israelites celebrated the Passover and remembered they were God's redeemed people, victory was secured. For this reason the manna from heaven stopped the day after the celebration. They were to eat the produce of Canaan. The victory was theirs before their first battle!

God freed me from strife and competitiveness in ministry when I found my significance in His love rather than in the approval of others.

WHOM DO I SERVE?—COMPLY WITH YOUR CAPTAIN

When we know who we are not and who we are, we may then answer the third question raised by Joshua 5: "Whom do I serve?" When the Israelites completed the circumcision and the Passover, Joshua met the Commander of the Lord's army near Jericho. Joshua asked Him, "Are you for us or for our enemies?" (Joshua 5:13). The reply was revealing: "Neither." God indicated that Joshua had asked the wrong question. The query should be reversed: Are we for the Lord, or are we not for Him? When the Captain of the host said, "Take off your sandals, for the place where you are standing is holy" (verse 15), Joshua knew exactly what He meant. In Egypt, where Joshua grew up, only one group of people did not wear sandals. These were the slaves who went about barefooted. To stand barefoot before the Lord means to be His slave. God is not our servant. We are His servants. God is the Captain, not we.

Until we circumcise our hearts and celebrate His victory, we cannot recognize Him as the Captain of our life and ministry. All too often, we live to serve ourselves—our selfish ambitions, our pride, and our security. To the extent we do so, our ministry will reflect our pride and self-centeredness. God cannot bless fully a work in which He is not the Commander-in-chief. When we allow God to take charge, His blessing flows like mighty living water.

This has been our experience at Faith Community Baptist Church. As I reflect upon the grace of the Lord in FCBC during the last several years, the Lord has impressed me with four major factors that have contributed to the phenomenal growth of this local congregation. These factors are (1) a clear vision and strategy for growth, (2) powerful visitations of the Holy Spirit in signs and wonders, (3) one strong and anointed leader, and (4) a cell church structure—a new wineskin. The rest of the book will discuss these factors at length. Here I simply affirm that FCBC has learned to soar with eagle's wings because we are a community of people who know who we are not, who we are, and whom we serve.

Two

RETHINKING THE WINESKIN:

— What is the Cell Church? —

Anyone who is sensitive to the work of the Holy Spirit around the world today would admit that we are living in the most exciting days of human history.

There were times in my life when I wished I had lived in the days of Moses. I thought it would have been wonderful if I could stand next to this servant of the Lord as he parted the Red Sea. What a glorious sight to witness the salvation of the Lord for His people! Then there were times when I wished I had been a contemporary of Elijah. I would have given anything to see the display of God's power when the prophet called down fire from heaven at Mount Carmel. At other moments, I wanted to have lived in the days of Jesus. It would surely have been life changing to walk beside our Lord as He taught and served the people on the dusty roads of Palestine. I imagined being among the five thousand Jesus fed with five loaves and two fishes. How thrilling to hear when Jesus called out Lazarus from the tomb where he had been dead for four days, or to feel the power released by the Lord's words when He calmed the sea! Wouldn't it be exciting to live in the days of Christ!

Yet in the past decade of my ministry, I wake up every morning thanking God that I am alive today! There is no doubt we are living in unprecedented times. The Lord is weaving some major movements of the Spirit on a global scale, preparing His church for a mighty end-time harvest. At least four significant world movements in the church of Jesus Christ can be identified:

1.   Holy Spirit Renewal

From the Pentecostal outpouring at the beginning of the 20th century to the charismatic movement to the "third wave" of the Holy Spirit and beyond, God is anointing the church to preach the gospel with signs and wonders. The Lord is visiting His people with His manifested presence. There is growing understanding that we must have both the Word of God and the works of God through His Spirit to accomplish His tasks.

2.   World Missions Movement

As the church presses toward the end of the second millennium since Christ, belief is growing that the task of world evangelization could be completed by the dawn of the 21st century or shortly thereafter. The AD2000 & Beyond Movement and the Global Consultations on World Evangelization (GCOWE) are uniting the body of Christ around the mandate of the Great Commission.

3.   Global Prayer Movement

The Holy Spirit is drawing God's people to fervent prayer. While the church advances within the most unevangelized areas, the body of Christ has experienced spiritual warfare more intensely than before. Commitment to prayer is rising rapidly. This prayer movement unites the body of Christ around the throne of grace. It also has brought forth a new wave of repentance to the church. As the church encounters the forces of darkness in Satan's territory, the Lord is purging us of sin to make us sufficient for the task.

4. Cell Church Movement

Without seeking permission from any of His people, the Holy Spirit has been renewing the structure of the church over the last three decades. He is changing the wineskins of the church to enable it to contain a great outpouring of the Spirit in the last days. Specifically, cell churches all over the world are emerging capable of reaching cities and whole nations with the gospel.

In recent decades, the Lord has restored to the body of Christ the five-fold ministries of Ephesians 4:11–13, namely the apostle, prophet, evangelist, pastor, and teacher. Now as we approach the new millennium, there will be a fresh move of God, taking the church beyond the prophetic era and the apostolic era into the era of the saints! Recall that the Ephesians passage says the five-fold offices are for "the equipping of the saints for the work of ministry" (verse 12, NKJV). In this era of the saints, the people of God will be released into the world as powerful, Spirit-filled, and well-equipped servants of the Lord to complete the task of world evangelization. The height of the cell church movement looms just ahead!

I believe the cell church is God's design to make His church capable of equipping and mobilizing every member for the work of the ministry. The cell church provides the structure by which "the whole body, joined and held together by every supporting ligament, grows and builds itself up in love, as each part does its work" (Ephesians 4:16).

PREREQUISITES FOR THE CELL CHURCH

Before giving a description of the cell church and its underlying principles, it is important to point out some prerequisites for any church considering taking on this model. Transitioning into a cell church is a major project for any traditional, program-based congregation, since it involves significant paradigm shifts in the way we think. Having worked with many churches around the world, I have come to recognize some fundamental conditions that must be met before a local congregation can become an effective cell church. These determine the environment absolutely needed for the renewal of the wineskin.

There are at least three prerequisites for successful transition to the cell church model: (1) commitment to a clear vision and strategy for growth, (2) reliance on the supernatural work of the Holy Spirit, and (3) a strong and God-anointed leader. Each of these points will be expanded in a later chapter of this book.

1.   Commitment to Clear Vision and Strategy for Growth

The cell church structure is not a quick fix for an ailing church. In fact, the challenge of implementing the cell church is more demanding than anything I have ever embarked upon.

For years I successfully pastored a traditional Baptist church. It was relatively easy to organize the church around worship services, Sunday school classes and various fellowships for various age groups. Most of the activities centered on teaching within a classroom. The biggest challenge most of the time was to make a good presentation, be it a sermon or a class lesson.

The situation is far more demanding in a cell church. When people are organized into small groups, they experience community life. Real problems in their lives begin to surface because cell members have no place to hide. Working through these life issues in the cells presents a major challenge. Also, these cells are continuously encouraged to grow and multiply. The task of equipping both members and leaders to ensure sustained growth is never-ending.

Moreover, every member in a cell church is called upon to give and serve sacrificially. To do so, the congregation must be consumed by a clear vision and strategy that they believe are of the Lord. Only then will they be willing to pay the price. The cell church structure is merely a strategy for growth. Unless both the pastor and the people are committed to a divinely inspired vision to win their community for Christ by reaching the lost, they will shrink from the high cost of functioning as a cell church.

Faith Community Baptist Church has a clear vision and strategy that the members share. This common viewpoint has resulted in great commitment to the cell structure as the means by which the vision is fulfilled. Our united outlook and our dedication to cells, despite the costs, come because the vision God has given us for growth and outreach to the lost is not something we possess but something that possesses us. We have heard from God, and this revelation motivates us to press on toward His goals. As Proverbs 29:18 (KJV) reminds us, "Where there is no vision, the people perish...."

A good vision from God does two things: It unites, and it divides. It firmly unites those who catch the vision and commit their lives to it. But it also divides those who do not share the vision, because they cannot remain long among the group moving ahead with what God has showed them. A church united in its God-inspired purpose will see its members willing to give their lives for the vision.

2. Reliance on the Supernatural Work of the Holy Spirit

Many have asked me if it is possible to have a cell church that is not charismatic. While I do not like to take on any labels, I would unequivocally state that without moving in the life and power of the Spirit, it would be impossible to have a dynamic cell church. A whole chapter later in this book is devoted to this subject. Suffice it to say here that a cell without the life of the Spirit is a dead cell. Cell members without the Spirit's power would burn out from the demands of the cell structure. When members do not exercise the supernatural gifts of the Holy Spirit, the cell meeting quickly becomes just another Bible study— or worse, a superficial social gathering of Christians. True body life is experienced only when members give room for the work of the Spirit and know how to minister to one another with the Spirit's anointing.

Furthermore, growth in the cell church often comes through power encounters with the Lord, who lives among His people. When God is alive and manifest in our cell meetings, the unsaved are attracted and begin to move in the flow of the living water. The apostle Paul says, "My message and my preaching were not with wise and persuasive words, but with a demonstration of the Spirit's power" (1 Corinthians 2:4). The growth of FCBC can be traced to the mighty visitations of the Holy Spirit in the life of the church. The cell structure has been the vehicle through which the anointing of the Spirit is released to every member in the cells.

3. A Strong and God-Anointed Leader

A cell church is structured like the military. Every cell represents a fighting unit for the kingdom of God. Like a mighty army, the cell church strategizes to invade Satan's territory through aggressive evangelism. Every cell member goes through disciplined training to become an effective minister of the gospel. To accomplish this, the cell church must be led by one strong and God-anointed leader.

The growth of FCBC is clearly the work of God's grace through my life and leadership. The church has recognized my God-given leadership and has learned to trust and to follow it. They pray for me and release me, under God's anointing, to lead them. The result is a well-disciplined, well-coordinated, and highly effective team of soldiers organized into cells as the basic fighting unit of a spiritual army.

An anointed leader, burning with faith and passion for the purposes of God, stirs others to follow in the same path of total commitment. Believers are mobilized and motivated to respond when their leader lays out the vision. The key lies not in the leader personally, but in the anointing of God on his or her life. A church without strong, anointed leadership suffers.

I will argue this point passionately in chapter 6 of this book. In my exposure to the cell church, I have found no exception: Every fast-growing cell church around the world has one strongly anointed person as its leader.

WHAT IS THE CELL CHURCH?

I would like to define the cell church with the following statements:

1. In the cell group church, the cell is the church.
2. In the cell group church, every cell multiplies or plants new cells by evangelism.
3. The cells in the cell group church are well structured for close supervision.
4. Cells are linked together in congregations.
5. Cells come together in celebration under one leadership.

Let's look at each point in turn.

1. The Cell is the Church.

During the last several years, Faith Community Baptist Church has organized an annual International Conference on Cell Group Churches. Thousands from around the world have come to learn the principles and operations of a cell group church. Every year, I begin the conference with a statement that has become a major landmark of my teaching on the subject. My statement is this: "There is a heaven and earth difference—an east and west difference—between a *church with cells* and a *cell group church.*"

Just about every church in the world has some kind of small groups. These may include Bible study groups, fellowship groups, counseling/therapy groups, prayer groups, and many others. Such churches, however, are churches with cells, rather than cell churches. The major difference between the former and the latter is a structural one. Hence, there is a *fundamental,* not a *superficial,* difference between them.

In a church with cells, the cell ministry is only a department within the total ministry of the church. Members of the church have many options. They may choose to serve in the missions department or the prayer department or the Christian education department or the fellowship department. They can choose between the Sunday school and the adult fellowship. The cell ministry is just another one of the options in a church with cells.

The cell group church is quite different. In a cell group church, *the cell is the church.* There is no buffet menu of options open to members except that they be in a cell group. The cells, not just the worship services, become the open front door of the church. Every department of the church is designed to serve the cell ministry. Indeed, departments do not have any constituency of their own. No program of any department competes with the activities and functions of the cell. All resources of the church are designed to support the ministry of the cells. The cells, in turn, provide the structure through which members may become involved in various church programs.

We see such a structure operating in the early church. Acts 2:46–47 tells us that "Every day they continued to meet together in the temple courts. They broke bread in their homes and ate together with glad and sincere hearts, praising God and enjoying the favor of all the people. And the Lord added to their number daily those who were being saved." In this model, the church functions through Christian communities within the home.

In FCBC, no one may join any training program or Bible class if he or she is not a member of a cell. I have often been asked, "Pastor Khong, how do you provide pastoral care to members who worship with you on Sunday and who are not in a cell group?" My answer: "I do not provide pastoral care for them." The reason is simple. The church has invested heavily to establish a thriving network of care and support for every member through the cells. If members of the church want spiritual and pastoral care, they must make themselves available to the system set up for that purpose. When a person belongs to a cell, he or she is cared for spiritually, equipped for ministry, and mobilized for the preaching of the gospel. In short, the cell fulfills all the primary functions of the church.

2. The Cell Grows by Evangelism.

The cell is an open group, and every cell is expected to grow by evangelism. Each cell should multiply within 12 to 18 months as the result of winning people to Christ. If a cell functions for a long time without multiplying or planting another cell, the cell is deemed unhealthy. The leadership may choose to dismantle the group and place the members into other cells that are spiritually vibrant.

This principle spotlights a distinct difference between small groups in a traditional church and the cells in a cell group church. In the latter, the cells are prevented from becoming inward-focused. Every cell begins with evangelism as its ultimate goal. In the first meeting of every cell, the members by faith set a date by which time the group will birth another cell. This vision keeps them focused and motivated toward reaching the lost. They can birth another cell by multiplying the existing group when the size has grown beyond 15 people. Or they can plant another group by branching into a certain unchurched sector of the community. Every member in the cell receives systematic training to accomplish this goal.

Dr. Ralph W. Neighbour, Jr., pioneer cell church strategist, first enlightened me about this distinctive feature of the cell church around the world. I felt as though scales suddenly fell off my eyes. I saw that this focus on evangelism is how the cell church penetrates society proactively. The cells are not allowed to become self-centered and inward-looking. They remain in constant contact with the world so as to evangelize the people around them. This was what happened in the first century. As the 3,000 or more Christians moved from house to house breaking bread, worshiping God, and praying, "the Lord added to their number daily those who were being saved" (Acts 2:47).

Infiltrating Society

When I, brimming with excitement, first shared this concept with my leadership in Faith Community Baptist Church, they did not receive it so enthusiastically. I remember one leader saying, "Pastor, this idea of growing the cell groups is a Western concept. It is American. Westerners tend to be more extroverted. The cell members in that context will "gel" quickly and people will be attracted to the group. We Chinese tend to be more conservative. It takes a long time for us to open up to each other, not to mention outsiders. We cannot expect the cells to grow quickly in our context here in the East."

While I appreciated this concern, I realize now that the premise was a lie from the evil one. This became clear to me in recent years as I have had the privilege of sharing the cell concept to Western believers. From them I have often heard this response: "Pastor Khong, I believe that this idea of multiplying cells is a very Eastern concept. Only the Koreans, the Chinese, or the Singaporeans could do it. You see, Pastor Khong, people in the East are more communal in nature. You are able to work in a regimented community for a common purpose. We in the West are too individualistic for such a system to work!"

The fact is that the devil wants to trap Christians within the four walls of the church. Satan will oppose any effort to release Christians into the community. Criminals do not mind if police officers spend most of their time in the precinct station having meetings and training—so long as they do not roam the streets doing their job. In the same way, the evil one does not mind when we are preoccupied with meetings and training within the church, so long as we do not infiltrate society preaching the gospel! The church must accomplish our task of world evangelization. If our culture resists that, our culture must give way to the biblical mandate.

3. The Cells are Well Structured for Close Supervision.

Cell groups in the cell church structure are not independent "house churches" but basic Christian communities linked together to penetrate every area of our society. Approximately three to four cell groups cluster to form a sub-zone. A volunteer zone supervisor pastors these four cells and their cell leaders. Up to ten sub-zones network to create a zone of 300 to 600 people pastored by a full-time zone pastor. Five or more zones form a district, with a seasoned district pastor shepherding 1,500 or more people.

We see the same kind of supervisory system in Exodus 18:21, when Moses' father-in-law advised him to select capable leaders "and appoint them as officials over thousands, hundreds, fifties and tens."

This cell structure enables tight supervision by the leadership. In the cell church, relatively young Christians may serve in responsible leadership positions. This is possible because of the careful and strict supervision and mentoring provided on every level of leadership. Such a structure, with its effective leadership training, results in massive mobilization of the members.

4. Cells are Linked Together in Congregations.

While the cell is the church, the church is more than the cell. As mentioned earlier, the cells do not function independently. Each is linked with other cells to fulfill a greater vision. From the start, we created districts that were geographical (north, central, east, west) and generational (children, youth, military). These districts serve as the congregations of Faith Community Baptist Church.

The congregations serve a number of purposes:

a. They provide a wider network of relationships.

On the cell level, kinship is forged between the members. On the congregational level, broader relationships are established. While the cells multiply continuously, relationships among cell members in separate groups can be maintained on the level of the congregations.

Presently, FCBC has eight districts serving as congregations. Every Friday evening, FCBC has a prayer and praise service "sponsored" by one of the districts on a rotation basis. This means that every congregation meets once every eight weeks for a prayer meeting involving all its cells. For that particular week, all the cells in that district do not meet in the homes. Instead, they come to the main sanctuary for the prayer and praise service. In this way, the members of each district keep in touch with one another.

b. *They spell out the vision of the church in more*
    concrete terms.

The vision of FCBC is clearly cast, concretized, and communicated to every member of the church. The district further develops its own vision under the umbrella of the total vision of the church. In so doing, every member comes to understand his or her role within the overall direction of the church. On the district or congregational level, the district pastor shares the heartbeat and the challenges unique to the vision of that congregation, thus drawing members more deeply into the vision of the church.

c. *They allow for better management of the programs*
    of the church.

The reason we do not have a prayer meeting for every member of the church every week is to keep the number of weekly meetings to a minimum. Again, our focus remains on cells and their ministry. Every cell member is expected to be involved at least two nights a week. On one evening, everyone attends the cell meeting. On another evening, everyone participates in some form of cell ministry. This may involve reaching out to the unsaved, or engaging in mutual care, discipleship, or leadership training.

Since each congregation develops its own vision in line with the overall vision of the church, every district learns to manage its own programs that are designed to achieve the district objectives and goals. In the annual planning process of FCBC, cell leaders, zone supervisors, and zone pastors meet with their district pastors to plan the programs of the coming year, given the overall direction for the church. This process yields a much greater level of ownership and therefore participation in fulfilling the vision of FCBC.

5. All Cells Come Together in Weekly Celebrations.

Not only do the cells meet periodically as congregations in districts, they also come together in one place for weekly celebrations. Ideally, this should be a place where everyone gathers to celebrate the Lord and His works among the people. In FCBC, we do this weekly in nine worship services, meeting in two places linked together by direct video broadcasting. Once every quarter, the church rents an indoor sports stadium with a capacity for 12,000 people for an exciting gathering of every cell.

The celebration serves the following functions:

a. It provides a place for vision-casting by apostolic leadership.

A successful, growing cell church is always led by apostolic leadership. In the weekly celebrations, the apostolic leader brings a word from the Lord concerning what God is doing among His people. This realigns the whole church to God's vision, and rekindles a fresh enthusiasm for and commitment to the vision of the church.

b. It models Welcome, Worship, Works, and Word for the cells.

Our cell meetings are divided into four segments: Welcome, Worship, Works, and Word. (These "Four W's" are described at the beginning of the next chapter.) The weekly celebrations model for the cells what these components should be like. The worship on the weekend sets the pace for the cells. The cells discuss the Word of God preached on the weekend. The members of the cells talk about their involvement in the work of the ministry available to every person in the church, as it is pointed out in the weekly celebration times. This means the cell meeting and the celebration reinforce one another in terms of worship, teaching, and service.

c. It brings unity to the whole movement.

As was pointed out earlier, the cell church is not a collection of independent cells. While the cell is the church, the church is more than just cells. The weekend celebrations foster unity throughout the body and show that each cell is part of something bigger than itself. In this way the cells are joined together in one mighty movement of God committed to fulfill God's highest purposes for that community.

KEEPING THE CELL STRUCTURE PURE

One danger in the process of transitioning into a cell church is the temptation to revert to methods belonging to the old paradigm. Operating in a new paradigm presents an inherent challenge in that we do not have precedents from which to learn. When we encounter a problem in the process of change, the easiest solution is to activate one of the old familiar programs. We are good at using these old methods; most of us have been schooled in them all our lives. The program momentarily solves the problem. Each time we do this, however, we drift unconsciously back into the old paradigm. Let me give you one example from the mission field.

In January 1993, I was ministering in the Republic of Mongolia in -35°C temperature. Such freezing cold is unimaginable for someone who grew up in Singapore, where the temperature never gets below

+ 23°C. If not for a specific directive from God, I would not have taken the trip. Ulaanbaatar, the capital city, was still somewhat primitive. The electrical power failed three or four times a day. The average home had no telephone service. Communication took place by word of mouth.

While in Mongolia, I taught small groups of believers and leaders of this infant church about the cell ministry. They in turn passed the word around, and then more came to my apartment for instructions.

I left Ulaanbaatar with a heavy heart. Although I was glad I had obeyed the Lord in visiting Mongolia, I didn't know if my ministry would bear fruit within a young, immature, and somewhat divided church.

No news came from them for a long time. Then in the beginning of 1997, I was surprised by an urgent invitation from Ulaanbaatar to conduct a seminar on the cell church. Probing further, I discovered an amazing testimony that came as the direct fruit of my ministry there some four years before.

A Swedish missionary couple had sat through my teaching in Ulaanbaatar in 1993. Three weeks later, they left for Erdenet, the third largest city in Mongolia, with the purpose of planting a cell church. They brought along an 18-year-old girl, a new convert by the name of Baira. Within about four years, they established the largest indigenous church in Mongolia, with some 800 members, completely organized as a cell church according to my teaching. Their success stirred up much interest within the churches in Ulaanbaatar to learn more about the cell ministry.

This time in 1997, I spoke to a group of about 200 leaders in the capital city. Baira sat attentively through my teaching on the principles of the cell church. This 22-year-old girl was now the acting senior pastor of the church in Erdenet. At the end of my first session, she came to me with tears in her eyes. She felt most convicted by the distinction I made between a "church with cells" and a "cell church."

She said, "Pastor Lawrence, I now know the reason why my church has stopped growing in the past year. You see, we have moved from being a cell church to becoming a church with cells. Many missionaries have come to my city to introduce many new programs. Some told us to run youth meetings on Saturday afternoons. Others said we should have one evening devoted to visitation of new members. Yet others insisted that no respectable church should be without a mid-week prayer meeting. Today, in my church, we have a meeting almost every evening of the week. The cell group meeting is only one among many activities. No wonder the cell groups have stopped multiplying."

I was impressed by the insight Baira gained concerning the cell church. During my visit to Mongolia in 1993, I could not have explained to the believers what it meant to be a "church with cells." The church was so new that they had no background to draw from. This young pastor in Erdenet had to discover for herself the futility of the traditional church with cells, in comparison to the explosive power of a pure cell church.

In the next chapter we will take a closer look at the cell agenda and examine the principles and strengths of the cell church.

Three

RULES FOR THE NEW WINESKIN:

— Principles of the Cell Church —

If you have ever driven on the opposite side of the road when traveling internationally, you know the sense of disorientation. First, you go to the wrong side of the car to get into the driver's seat. Then you notice that, while the accelerator is still on the right, the hand controls are completely backwards. At the street corner you hit what you take to be the turn signal, and your wind screen wipers begin scraping across the glass. Turns get tricky, especially when a traffic island lies in the middle of the road. And heaven help you if you have to deal with a manual shift transmission on top of everything! Any situation requiring a quick reaction spells trouble, because all your instincts are wrong.

Coming out of a traditional, program-based church into the cell church model can prompt similar initial reactions. The cell church represents a new paradigm in thinking about the way we do church. Stepping into a new paradigm can be compared to entering a brand-new world. In this "new world," the rules of operation have changed completely. Methods and programs that worked in the past can no longer be used. New ways of doing things must be adopted.

Initially, confusion reigns when trying to figure out how things work. That's why it is important to take those first baby steps by following what others have already done successfully. Nevertheless, even when simply copying others, it is imperative to grapple personally with the basic principles of the cell church.

These principles serve, in effect, as "rules" for the new wineskin. This chapter explores these rules or principles. While the forms may be adapted to changing situations, the rules remain unchanged. Over the years, these principles have become foundations for the ministry at Faith Community Baptist Church. They provide a compass that helps churches keep their bearings while steering through the uncharted waters of transitioning into a cell church.

THE CELL AGENDA

Before exploring the principles of the cell church, it is important to describe the cell agenda. The cell is the smallest structural unit of the cell church. Cell meetings seek to accomplish two goals: edification and evangelism.

The first purpose of the cell meeting is edification of the cell members. In 1 Corinthians 14:26 (NAS), the apostle Paul says, "What is the outcome then, brethren? When you assemble, each one has a psalm, has a teaching, has a revelation, has a tongue, has an interpretation. Let all things be done for edification." The cell meeting goes beyond just a Bible study or a "sharing and caring" time. When we meet, we expect the Lord to move among us, releasing His revelation, His word, and His power to touch our lives. We desire and look for an encounter with the living God. Not only are our minds informed, our emotions touched, and our wills strengthened, the Spirit of God also touches the spirit of every person.

The second purpose of the cell meeting is evangelism. Cells engage in much warfare prayer over the lives of the unsaved. Every person is accountable to the group for living out an evangelistic lifestyle. The cell meeting is conducted in such a way that unbelievers invited to attend will feel at home in the meeting. As a result, the non-Christian in a cell meeting will see the reality of God's presence and exclaim, "God is really among you!" (1 Corinthians 14:25b).

At Faith Community Baptist Church, we pursue the twin goals of edification and evangelism in the cell meeting by means of the "Four W's." The Four W's incorporate the four stages of the cell meeting, namely Welcome, Worship, Works, and Word.

1. Welcome

During the time of welcome, the group participates in an "icebreaker." This is a light-hearted activity that helps to thaw frozen relationships at the beginning of the meeting. Every effort is made to put each person at ease and facilitate relationships with one another. During this time, newcomers receive a warm welcome and introduction to the whole group. If the cell has newly formed, the welcome time may stretch to half an hour or longer in the first few meetings, but shortens quickly to about five or ten minutes. Even for groups that have met together for months, the "icebreaker" has proved indispensable to gaining momentum and preparing people for greater participation in the meeting.

2. Worship

Worship is most the powerful part of the cell meeting. Once worship begins, all attention focuses upon the Lord. Worship is not a time to "sing a few songs while we wait for latecomers." Rather, it expresses our ministry unto the Lord. We expect to worship down the manifested presence of God in every meeting. Cells spend at least half an hour worshiping and delighting in the Lord.

As the presence of the Lord grows in the midst of the worship, He begins to speak to His people in prophetic utterances. Revelations and words of knowledge surface needs within the lives of the people gathered. The cell members respond to God's leadership as they minister to one another with the gifts of the Holy Spirit. It is not uncommon for demons residing in the lives of some to manifest. Cell members have been trained to deal appropriately with this situation. They have learned to cast out evil spirits authoritatively without giving the spirits undue attention. All focus must remain upon the Lord. An awesome sense of His presence typically fills the room where the cell meets.

3. Works

At the height of ministering to the Lord and to one another, the cell engages in spiritual warfare. The meeting then enters into the Works stage. At this time, we focus on the unsaved friends in our lives. Each cell member keeps a list of names of unbelievers for whom they are praying. The cell prays over these names, asking for God's grace and mercy to convict their hearts of their need for the Lord.

Often the cell prays for an upcoming "harvest event." A harvest event is an evangelistic meeting that may be organized on the cell, congregation, or celebration level. If the cell is closely involved in one of these events, the members may take some time to discuss related administrative details. In addition, most cells have a small group of members conducting a special cell-planting project, such as in an office or a secondary school. The Works stage of the meeting provides opportunity for them to update the cell about the progress of the outreach and solicit prayer. In summary, this stage is a time when the cell prays for the lost and makes plans to reach them as God directs.

4. Word

While the Works stage directs the hearts of cell members toward the lost, the Word stage refocuses them on God's dealings in their lives. In Faith Community Baptist Church, the cells discuss the biblical passage used as the text for the previous week's sermon. This focus gives more mileage to the message the Lord has given to His people.

Each week, the district pastors take turns preparing the Four W's for that week's cell meetings. Everything, from Welcome to Works, draws cell members back to the Word in an integrated whole. This final stage of the cell meeting can become open-ended. Sometimes members gather in twos or threes for deeper sharing. They may also talk openly together as a whole cell. Such sharing leads again to prayer and ministry to one another. The cell leaders receive constant reminders that the main agenda of the cell is not the program but people. Each cell meeting ends with praying for blessings upon each other in light of the biblical teaching.

THE PRINCIPLES AND STRENGTHS OF THE CELL CHURCH

Since 1988, Faith Community Baptist Church has learned and practiced the fundamental principles of the cell church. What I am about to share is of utmost importance to those venturing out to renew the wineskin of the church. Some pastors return to Singapore every year for our International Conference on Cell Group Churches just to get fresh input on cell church principles. Indeed, the more experience one gains in the cell church ministry, the more one understands and appreciates these principles, because they serve as the rules of operation in this new paradigm. Following them is the reason the cell church has been so effective in both changing lives and reaching out with the gospel.

One of the pitfalls in the process of transitioning into a cell church is that we tend to slip back into our old ways of doing things, because we have no precedents to help us deal with problems in the new paradigm. We naturally revert to the patterns we are used to, importing something that has worked for us in the past from the traditional, program-based structure. This decision will often succeed initially because we are expert in these methods. If we do this long enough, however, we will drift right back into the old system, short-circuiting the process of growth.

Because the principles of the cell church undergird everything the church does, we must maintain commitment to them in order to grow and win our communities for Christ. The following principles are the imperatives of the cell church structure:

1. Learning takes place through experiences in the cells.
2. Leaders are chosen and equipped through the cells.
3. Every member must be mobilized through the cells.
4. Cells penetrate the community through "body evangelism."
5. Cells experience body life through the gifts of the Holy Spirit.
6. All functions of the church are integrated within the cells.

In the rest of this chapter we will examine each of these principles in depth.

1. Learning Takes Place Through Experiences in the Cells.

One of the distinctives of the cell church is the way truths are communicated. In the cell church, learning takes place through experiences within the community of the cells. The Bible clearly tells us to be "doers of the word, and not hearers only, deceiving your own selves" (James 1:22, KJV). From the Lord's perspective, a person has not learned a spiritual truth until he or she puts it into practice. This means that authentic learning must come through an experience of spiritual realities. The community of the cell provides an environment where its members experience truth for themselves.

Three Domains of Learning

Experts in education tell us there are three domains of learning. The first domain is the cognitive. In this domain, a person simply acquires knowledge. Such knowledge is transmitted typically in a classroom by means of a lecture. Cognitive knowledge rarely affects the life of the student. It is simply stored in the mind as part of the databank of knowledge.

The second domain of learning is the psychomotor. In this domain, a person acquires a skill. Such learning comes in a workshop environment where coaching takes place. For example, when I take tennis lessons, I do not go to a classroom and listen to my trainer deliver a lecture on tennis. Rather, my coach feeds me baskets of tennis balls on the court so I can practice. I receive feedback as I rehearse the required actions again and again until the skill is acquired.

Finally, the third domain of learning is the affective. This is the level of the heart, where true learning takes place. In this domain, values and lives are changed.

Let's suppose I hear a lecture on how to share the "Four Spiritual Laws" as a means of evangelism. At the end of the class, I have cognitively learned this method of gospel presentation. I may not be able to use it competently, however, since I have not yet practiced and acquired the skills. I need someone to take me out to the streets, demonstrate using this wonderful tool for evangelism, then watch me as I use it myself, and give me feedback.

Nevertheless, I may learn about and even acquire the skill of using this tool and still never use it! Why? My value system has not yet changed. Understanding the "Four Spiritual Laws" and knowing how to use this tool will accomplish nothing if I have no interest in using it because I don't really care whether others come to know the Lord.

The Fallacy of Cognitive Learning

The church in today's world often falls into the trap of teaching on only the cognitive level. We have bought into the philosophy that knowledge itself is life-changing—while, ironically, the Bible says, "knowledge puffs up . . ." (1 Corinthians 8:1). This worldview causes us to run a church the way we run a school. People are divided into age groups and assigned to classes. What do we do with new converts? We give them a follow-up package and stick them into a class! I agree with Dr. Howard Hendricks, my professor at Dallas Theological Seminary, who said, "Most Christians are like poor photographs. We are overexposed and underdeveloped."

One of the greatest objections to our transition into the cell church structure at Faith Community Baptist Church has been the concern that we provide insufficient teaching of the Bible. Since the cell meeting is not a Bible study, observers may fear that the members do not get strongly built up in the Word of God, resulting in shallow and ignorant Christians. This reflects more "old paradigm" thinking.

Many people have the misconception that "solid" or "deep" Bible study consists of the ability to analyze the text, identify the argument of a passage, and preferably understand the words in the original language. Christians love to go from class to class or seminar to seminar listening to Bible teachers give a "new angle" on a familiar passage. For years, I thought that the "solid food" of Hebrews 5:14 referred to Greek and Hebrew exegesis. Now I realize that "solid food" speaks not so much of the knowledge of the Word but of the constant application of the Word. Those who practice this, as the verse says, "have trained themselves to distinguish good from evil."

If "solid food" meant advanced exegesis and textual analysis, uneducated Christians would be incapable of receiving it. That, my friend, comprises more than 80 percent of the world's population! No wonder Christianity in many cultures draws only those who are educated and middle-class. At FCBC, we believe that the Bible is written for ordinary folks. Obedience to God's Word, not just an understanding of it, determines depth in the knowledge of the truth. One young Christian may practice five biblical truths he has learned that year, while another who has been taught 50 important truths from the Bible is not practicing any. I believe the former represents a stronger Christian than the latter.

Value Changes Through the Cells

In Faith Community Baptist Church, we aim for value changes in the lives of our people. Value change takes place when a person's value system is challenged by someone else's differing value. The person then must choose: Do I hold on to my own values, or do I yield to the differing values? This experience begins a process of change and growth. Affective learning takes place only through such experiences. These experiences must reinforce the truths that have been communicated cognitively.

The cell, the basic unit of Christian community, provides the environment for affective learning. Let's look at an individual example. James was a successful businessman. He had been won to the Lord as a result of a crisis in his business. As a spiritual infant, James maintained many of his unethical business practices. In his thinking, he could not envision a businessman being totally honest and yet successful. Although he aspired toward the biblical standard of integrity, he believed it impossible to practice in real life.

James met Mark in his cell group and was intrigued to discover that Mark, too, was a successful businessman. Mark was assigned to be his sponsor, someone who helps a new Christian through basic equipping in the cell. Over the next few months, Mark met with James regularly. As they came to know each other well, James recognized that Mark was a man of high integrity. Mark shared with him many testimonies of how the Lord had honored him and his business because of his complete honesty toward his clients. James' value system was challenged and began to change. Today, James helps other Christian businessmen to stand firm on Christian principles in the business world.

Life change occurs through confrontations with one's value system. Such confrontations take place naturally as people rub shoulders with one another in the life of a cell. This is one reason the cell church brings about powerful change and growth in the lives of its members.

From Knowledge to Experience

Cell leaders keep this principle in mind when discussing the Sunday sermon during the Word stage of the cell meeting. Knowledge of the specific biblical passage has been imparted cognitively. Then in the cell, every member exposes his or her value system in the light of God's truth. Mutual love and acceptance draw each person to share honestly about successes and failures. As people become real with one another, their hearts are touched at the deepest level. They have no place to hide in this basic Christian community. Yet, in such an environment of love, there is no need to hide. You might say the cell meeting is not a Bible study but a "body" study in spiritual values for living.

As a rule, when FCBC leadership wants to inculcate a certain spiritual lifestyle in the church, we do not simply organize a class or seminar, even if we have the best speaker available. We may do that, but we always go one step beyond. We ask ourselves, "What experiences can we design into the cell life so that this biblical value is caught?"

One example is the way we teach evangelism. Chapter 7 will discuss this in detail. Suffice it to mention that we have designed "evangelism cycles" into the life of the cells so that every member is constantly in an "evangelistic environment." They literally talk, eat, sleep, and dream evangelism! This focus naturally brings every new Christian in the cell into an evangelistic lifestyle. New believers begin to share Christ even before they have had any formal teaching and training on how to do so.

We follow this principle in every discipline of the Christian faith, including prayer, Bible reading, Christian family life, and so on. In FCBC, we seek to preclude any opportunity for our people to be mere hearers and not doers of the word. This principle empowers the cell church to change lives through the Christian community.

2. Leaders are Chosen and Equipped Through the Cells.

The cell structure provides a highly effective means of choosing and equipping leaders for ministry. One of the greatest challenges most churches face is raising good leaders. In a typical church, the leadership base remains essentially unchanged even when the congregation begins to grow. Soon heavy pressure builds on the small team of people who must carry the increasing ministry load. Meanwhile the rest of the members seem quite willing to watch the small band of committed leaders work themselves into the ground. In so doing, these inactive majorities become "spiritually retarded." Their lives remain unfruitful for the Lord.

The cell church takes seriously the responsibility of entrusting the truth to reliable people who will also be qualified to teach others (see 2 Timothy 2:2). Training leaders ranks high in the priority of a cell church. In Faith Community Baptist Church, we have about 700 cells, each with cell leaders and cell "interns." A cell intern is someone in training to be the cell leader of a new group when the existing cell multiplies. In addition, some 200 zone supervisors serve as lay leaders overseeing three or four cells each. FCBC now has some 250 paid staff members, of whom more than 120 are pastors. These include zone pastors, district pastors, and directors of ministry. Almost all of these have been raised internally through the cell structure.

Leaders are Chosen in the Cells

The cell system provides a structure in which leaders can surface naturally—or perhaps, shall I say, "supernaturally." As Christians live in community, supernatural gifting surfaces naturally. Leaders become recognized and affirmed by the body of believers. With no place to hide in the basic Christian community of a cell, the genuineness of spirituality, the authenticity of God's calling, as well as the depth of commitment to the church vision can all be identified easily in this environment. The result is a growing number of leaders sincerely following the will of God in their personal lives and solidly behind the vision of the church.

I am careful not to allow anyone into leadership who has not come through the rank and file of cell life. It does not matter if the person served as deacon or pastor of another congregation before joining us. In fact, I am more cautious with leaders of other churches who join us, because I want to be sure they unlearn their old paradigm thinking before they are mobilized in our church on any level of leadership. The best way to do this is to have them grow through the equipping system of the cell structure. By the time someone is trained as a cell leader, he or she will have been observed within the life of a cell. Every zone supervisor, before appointment, will have multiplied a cell group at least twice as a cell leader. Then the zone pastors and district pastors will have further opportunity to test this person's heart for the Lord and commitment to the vision of the church.

When a person heeds the call of God to full-time ministry, either as a zone pastor or a missionary in our church, the leadership will have observed this person's life and ministry for a number of years. This process has ensured that we have the best men and women as full-time pastors of the church. As evidence, since 1988 there has been a turnover of no more than five people on a team of some 150 pastors!

Training of Leaders is a Built-in Process

The cell system works only to the extent that new leaders emerge. If every cell multiplies after 12 months, the number of cell leaders must be double every year. This can happen only when leadership training is a built-in process within the cell structure. The process of leadership training becomes both the strength as well as the challenge of the cell church.

Right from the beginning, I saw this as key. Unless leaders are trained through the cell structure, sustained growth becomes unattainable. It is impossible to draw from an external pool of leaders to service such a dynamically growing structure. It must be part and parcel of the system. A growing cell church demands machinery that equips every cell member for ministry in order that leaders can surface at a pace commensurate to the growth.

I spent many years designing a basic equipping system for every person in the cell. Chapter 9 will give details on this subject. In Faith Community Baptist Church, we begin a leadership training process at the lowest level of the membership by training "sponsors" to help new believers. These sponsors are themselves young Christians who have worked through some basic material on Christian growth. We quickly deploy them to help others through the same materials. In addition, each cell leader earmarks one or two cell interns whom they train to become leaders when the cell multiplies.

Equipping Stations at Each Level

FCBC's training department is called TESS, which stands for TOUCH Equipping Station System. We call the different stages of training "equipping stations" to show that they are part of the process and not the end. Just as with train stations or filling stations, no one stays there for good—they are only a means to get on with the journey. In the same way, we try to make sure that training or attending classes does not become an end in itself.

TESS has done a detailed job analysis of every leadership task in the cell church, from cell leader, zone supervisor, zone pastor, and district pastor to senior pastor. With a clear job description for every task, we design training processes to equip leaders for each level of ministry.

Training, clearly, is fundamental to the success of the cell church. It must focus on equipping leaders to do their jobs at every level. In the cell structure, we take seriously the mandate of Scripture given in 2 Timothy 2:2, "And the things you have heard me say in the presence of many witnesses entrust to reliable men who will also be qualified to teach others."

Churches transitioning to the cell church model need to face the reality that not all of the people mobilized for ministry will serve as capably as the one doing the training or mentoring, especially in the early stages. Leaders at every level must resist the temptation to do the work themselves rather than take the time and effort to raise up and release others into kingdom responsibilities. The cell church will sustain growth only through continual equipping of the saints for the work of ministry.

3. Every Member Must Be Mobilized Through the Cells.

A third major principle of the cell church is the mobilization of every member for ministry. Cell churches provide a tremendous structure within which this can happen. Because of this pattern and practice, many members hear and respond to the call of God to full-time service. Faith Community Baptist Church, as a result, enjoys a high level of commitment from both full-time and volunteer leaders.

Every Believer is a Minister

One reason for the effectiveness of the cell church structure is its ability to facilitate ministry mobilization of each believer. Traditional structures have built-in limitations to the mobilization process, because only so many vacancies exist for Sunday school superintendents, choir directors, missions board members, and so on. The growing cell church, in contrast, always has need for more cell leaders, zone supervisors, zone pastors, and so on.

Few would refute the truth of the axiom, "Every believer is a minister." The structure of the traditional church, however, does not permit the outworking of this conviction. Hence, it remains at best a hoped-for ideal, at worst an empty platitude that no one takes seriously. The cell church not only takes this truth seriously, it actually puts it into practice. In the cell church, the cells are mobilized to fulfill every task required of the church. As a result, every member gets plunged into ministry.

To begin with, every member becomes thoroughly involved in caring for others. Today, I as the senior pastor of Faith Community

Baptist Church do not visit the sick in the hospital, dedicate infants, or even perform baptisms. These ministries are all done by members of the cells who, because they are closer to the recipients, can provide better service than the pastors of the church. Whenever a cell member or family member is hospitalized, the whole cell gathers in the hospital room. In the case of serious illness, cell members take turns staying with the family, sometimes 24 hours a day. Infant dedication takes place in the cell meetings, when grandparents, uncles, and aunts are invited to this special occasion. This pattern provides powerful opportunities for Christian witness. The cell leader, together with the zone supervisor, baptizes new converts from that cell during the weekend worship services. A person who lives in the community of the cells is fully mobilized as a minister of the gospel.

Many are Called into Full-Time Ministry

As members get released into ministry, many sense the call to career ministry or missions. I believe God continually calls workers into the mighty harvest, yet few hear His summons because many churches encourage believers to sit and soak. Their hearts do not get stirred with excitement toward the ministry of changing lives with the gospel of Christ.

In Faith Community Baptist Church, many zone supervisors spend considerable time winning their community to Christ and shepherding new believers. Their ministry gives them a far greater sense of fulfillment than their successful career, so they do not find it difficult to respond to the call of the Holy Spirit to full-time ministry. Most of the more than 120 paid pastoral staff at FCBC, including many of the top-level pastors, gave up secular jobs and careers to join our team. Since FCBC's launch, we have sent out more than 20 career missionaries, raised within the church, to plant churches within the 10/40 Window. (This region, between 10 and 40 degrees north latitude and stretching from West Africa through East Asia, is home to the world's least evangelized peoples.) The great sense of commitment to the work of the kingdom felt by so many of our people comes from being mobilized as ministers of the gospel early in their Christian lives.

4. Cells Penetrate the Community Through "Body Evangelism."

This is the most powerful principle of the cell church. Body evangelism enables the cell church to reach the community effectively with the gospel of Jesus Christ. Part of chapter 7 delves into this principle in greater detail. Here let me point out just two important truths on this subject.

The Cell Church Penetrates the Community with the Gospel

The Lord has commissioned us to go to all people groups to share the gospel. Traditionally, by contrast, the body of Christ has devised programs and developed structures in order to invite the world to come to our churches.

The cell church is set up as a *Go* structure rather than a *Come* structure. That's how the early church shook the whole of Jerusalem with the gospel. The believers continually worshiped the Lord, prayed, and broke bread in homes. They brought the church to the people. It was indeed a "church without walls."

We have all heard godly pastors tell their congregations, "If you love the Lord, you should be at the church every time the door is open." This thinking has trapped believers within the confines of a building. It represents, I believe, a major deception of the evil one. If the devil cannot stop us from loving God and living for Him, he simply neutralizes our spiritual influence by keeping our primary expressions of these priorities within religious buildings. As I pointed out in the previous chapter, criminals face no threat from the police as long as officers remain safely confined within the precinct stations. They can busy themselves with seminars on criminology or practice sessions to sharpen their shooting skills, but as long as they stay off the streets, criminals can continue to do as they please.

To counter this demonic strategy, the cell church tears down the dividing walls between believers and the unsaved. It brings the church to the people. The cell meetings serve as open doors to give non-Christians contact with Christians in a natural, unthreatening setting. Rather than exclusive Bible studies or discipleship groups, the cells are living communities where unbelievers can find God.

The Cell Church Offers Unbelievers an Alternate Community Where God is Alive

Many evangelistic programs are based on communication of a set of truths regarding the gospel, typically some form of a booklet or a memorized presentation. This approach reflects a Western mindset that believes one must inform the mind in order to transform the heart. Human experience, however, shows the fallacy of this premise. Convictions of the heart, especially religious ones, are shaped much more by relationships than by knowledge.

Consider one example. In Brazil, soccer is almost a religion. During the World Cup games, the whole country comes to a standstill. The metropolis of São Paulo becomes a ghost town as people stay glued to their radios and televisions. While I was ministering in São Paulo, I asked the audience to raise their hands if they liked soccer. Virtually every hand lifted. Then I followed with a second question: "Why do you like soccer?" A moment of silence ensued. "Do you like soccer because you have attended a seminar about it?" I proceeded to ask. The audience shook their heads, bewildered. "Or did you read a book about soccer that got you committed to the game?" Again, they shook their heads in vigorous denial. "Or perhaps you love soccer because your family members love soccer. Your friends love soccer. In fact, everybody in Brazil loves soccer. Right?" The audience then applauded in unequivocal agreement.

The fact is clear: The community to which a person belongs largely influences his or her commitment to a belief system.

I will never forget an experience early in my ministry. At the deathbed of an elderly man, I shared the gospel with him and his wife. Although the man, sadly, expressed little interest, his wife was quite receptive. Prayerfully, I walked her through the "Four Spiritual Laws." At the end of the presentation, I asked gently, "Madam, do you believe that you are a sinner?" With a sense of deep penitence, she replied in the affirmative. "Do you believe that Jesus Christ has died for your sins?" I continued. "Yes, I believe," she answered with certain conviction. By now, I was excited to see what the Holy Spirit was doing! With great anticipation I popped the question, "Are you willing to accept Jesus Christ as your personal Lord and Savior now?" She looked up and said, "No. I don't think so."

A wave of confusion passed over me. Again, I went through those standard questions, as I had been taught to do. Again, she answered "yes" to all except the last one. Somehow, although she believed in her need for the Lord Jesus Christ, she was unwilling to accept Him.

I added another question. "Madam, why are you not willing to give your life to the Lord right now?" She answered simply, "I cannot become a believer because my husband is not a believer."

My response to her answer was predictable. With an attitude typical of a Westerner (I consider myself to be one), I stressed that the decision to put one's faith in Christ is strictly personal. Each of us must take individual responsibility for our own commitment to Him. Emphatically, I underscored the importance of not allowing her husband to get in the way of her personal salvation.

A puzzled look now reflected on the woman's face. She said, "Pastor, let me try to understand this. If I have heard you correctly," she continued politely, "I would go to heaven when I die if I put my faith in Jesus."

"Absolutely!" I agreed.

"This means," she went on, with emotion in her voice, "my husband will go to hell if he dies without Jesus in his heart." I was taken aback by her straightforward statement. Sensitively, I assured her that as long as her husband had not breathed his last, the door of salvation remained open to him.

Then came this statement that completely stunned me. With a great sense of sincerity, she said, "Pastor, if my husband would go to hell after his death, how could I, as his wife, forsake him and go to heaven alone?"

My Western education had not prepared me for such a perspective. Theologically, I am certain that her statement came as a deception of the evil one. Yet as a Chinese, my culture tells me there is something very virtuous about what she said. It took me years before I fully understood the truth behind her words—that commitment to the Lord is never just a personal decision. It always occurs in the context of a community.

Finding Jesus in Community

Paul and Silas told the Philippian jailer, "Believe in the Lord Jesus, and you will be saved—you and your household" (Acts 16:31). In the same manner, Jesus did not tell the multitudes, "Accept me as your personal Savior and you will go to heaven when you die." Rather, Jesus came to offer an alternate community. He declared, "Repent, for the kingdom of heaven is near" (Matthew 4:17). Jesus presents to us a new community in which He reigns as king, a community where God is alive and His power is evident.

The best way to draw the unsaved into God's kingdom is for them to experience Him within the God-centered community of the cell. In order for them to be willing to risk strained or even severed relationships with their own community, they must be convinced that this alternate community provides loving and God-centered relationships filled with the presence and power of the Lord.

No wonder most outreach methods, including large evangelistic campaigns, confess to rather dismal retention rates of new believers. A new convert has no idea what the church is like. Some time after his decision to believe in Jesus, he is introduced to this group of strangers in a local church, who are now his brothers and sisters in Christ. In order to get involved with this newfound spiritual family, the young believer realizes he must inevitably distant himself from his own friends and even family members, both ideologically as well as relationally. Unprepared to handle this tension, he drops out of the Christian community.

In the cell church, the cell allows the unbeliever to check out this potential family before he ever makes a decision to trust Christ. As he gets to know his potential brothers and sisters, he can come to experience the reality of the gospel within this God-centered community. The cell offers him a gospel that is more than just a guarantee of personal salvation after death. The Good News of Jesus Christ includes the invitation to be part of a spiritual family with a spiritual purpose here on earth. Many within the cells of Faith Community Baptist Church have found this gospel compelling, and have made irrevocable decisions to follow the Lord.

This concept of community has helped me to understand the truth of Ephesians 5:25 concerning Christ giving His life for the church. Jesus died in order to leave behind a powerful and loving community that issues a convincing invitation to the world to become followers of Christ. This is what happens in the cells. When a believer experiences the power of the Lord in a cell, "he will fall down and worship God, exclaiming, 'God is really among you!'" (1 Corinthians 14:25b).

In summary, cell members are always open to unbelievers walking among them and tasting the life of the cell. The cells become the first-line contact with the unsaved. They provide an environment where unbelieving friends can experience the presence and power of

God. Above all, they offer themselves as a family of God to the unbelieving world searching for personal security and significance in a loving community.

5. Cells Experience Body Life Through the Gifts of the Holy Spirit.

In order for the cell to provide an environment where the presence and power of God can be experienced, every member of the cell must know how to move in the supernatural gifts of the Holy Spirit. This is not optional but essential. Only then can a cell provide both edification of the believers as well as an effective witness of the gospel to the unsaved.

We have clear scriptural foundation for this. In 1 Corinthians 14:26 we read, "What then shall we say, brothers? When you come together, everyone has a hymn, or a word of instruction, a revelation, a tongue or an interpretation. All of these must be done for the strengthening of the church." Paul gives instructions as to what must take place in each gathering of the church or the cell. "When you come together" suggests a normal assembly of believers rather than a special meeting. At such a regular gathering, the scripture instructs "everyone" to exercise spiritual gifts in order to edify one another. Verses 24 and 25, just before this, refer to a situation when an unbeliever is touched by the presence of God because everyone in the group is prophesying. The operation of spiritual gifts opens the heart of the non-Christian to the gospel!

Margaret, an unbeliever, was laid off from her job. In her disappointment and sense of rejection, she responded to the invitation of an FCBC cell member to a cell meeting on Friday evening. When Margaret arrived at the meeting, worship had already begun, leaving no opportunity for her to be introduced to the group. As the worship continued, a member of the cell received a word from the Lord concerning someone in the meeting who had lost her job and was in a state of deep anxiety. Margaret began to weep. The group prayed over her situation. A word from the Lord was released from another member that she would find a job in two weeks. Margaret was deeply touched by the presence of God in that meeting. She gave her life to the Lord two weeks later when she received an unexpected job offer.

In FCBC, we instruct the cell leaders to spend considerable time in prayer laying hold of God for the cell meetings and seeking His anointing. We believe that if God does not show up in power, the whole meeting will be a washout. When the cell meets, we expect God to speak supernaturally, to reveal the secrets of the heart, to expose sin, to bring light into darkness, and to work signs and wonders.

6. All Functions of the Church are Integrated Within the Cells.

The last principle of the cell church is integration. The cell church dynamically integrates the various functions of the church in a holistic balance. Since the cell is the church, every function of the church needs to be worked out on the level of the cell.

As a cell seeks to edify every member, the functions of prayer, Bible study, and spiritual gifts are developed and practiced in the group. As the cell endeavors to win friends and neighborhoods to Christ, the functions of spiritual warfare, sharing of the gospel, signs and wonders, as well as strategic intercession are implanted within the lives of the members. The cell church strategy provides a structure that fulfills all the tasks of the church effectively.

This model promotes integration and balance. The Western church tends to encourage specialization too early in the life of a new believer. Many use the concept of the diversity of gifts and callings as an excuse for a lack of fervent prayer, proactive evangelism, or even sacrificial giving. They may say, "That's not my gift; I feel a greater call to such-and-such other ministry." Certainly, some believers are called to a ministry of prayer and intercession. Others have special gifting in Bible teaching. Some will have a powerful ministry of evangelism. Yet every believer should be deeply committed to prayer, the Word, and the spread of the gospel. The cell provides an environment in which members develop and exercise all these spiritual disciplines.

The cell structure, therefore, enables the church to operate as a family, an organization, and an army at the same time. Within the cell life, deep spiritual family ties are established. The highly organized structure of supervision in the cell church also makes it a well-coordinated machine empowered to accomplish specific purposes. Then as the cell church takes the gospel into the community, with each cell a fit fighting unit, the church shows itself as a powerful army capturing territories for the kingdom of God.

A Four

REALIZING GOD'S PURPOSES:

— Vision and Strategy for the Cell Church —

The chicken and the pig got up one fine morning at Farmer Brown's barnyard, with the sun shining in a blue sky.

"What a lovely day!" the pig exclaimed. "And I'm starved. Let's have something to eat!"

"Great idea," the chicken agreed. "How about a nice ham-and-eggs breakfast?"

The pig was ready to agree—but then he thought it over. "You know, I have a problem," the pig said. "For you, that idea requires only a contribution. For me, it means total commitment!"

Like the vision of a ham-and-eggs breakfast for a pig, the vision of a cell church requires total commitment. As I mentioned in chapter 2, commitment to a clear vision and strategy for growth is one of at least three prerequisites for successful transition to the cell church model. "Where there is no vision, the people perish..." says Proverbs 29:18 (KJV). And without united commitment to the vision, the church cannot advance.

Vision involves the ability to look forward, beyond the immediate situation. One of the core values of Faith Community Baptist Church is stated this way: "We believe that God has called this church to fulfill a specific purpose for this nation and the world. Therefore, we are a vision-driven community of believers."

In this chapter I share FCBC's vision and strategy as an example of what can be done by churches pursuing the cell church model. I have no intention that other churches should adopt this vision. In fact, each church must hear from the Lord individually in order to discover, commit to, and pursue the unique vision to which God calls that congregation.

A VISION BIRTHS A PLAN

A church's vision should have three elements:

1. It must be impossible, apart from God's power. If it can be accomplished in human strength, the vision is not large enough. Most jaded unbelievers will find little to attract them to church unless they see things happening that can be explained only by the supernatural power of God.

2. It must be measurable. Otherwise, a church has no way to know whether the vision has been accomplished.

3. It must be practical. This point does not contradict the first. The vision must be "practically" impossible. The church must concretize the vision and spell out particular things to do that will move them toward their goal.

Visionary leaders see potential. They dream big dreams. They look at their own city and recognize how it can fulfill God's desire that it be a community reached and transformed for His kingdom. Apostolic leaders should have a vision not only for their church but for their city, their nation, and their world.

Churches and their leaders who seek growth must take three steps:

1. A vision for reaching the lost is needed. This goes beyond a vision merely to enlarge the church. The church must have eyes to see the lost unbelievers around them—who they are, where they are, how they can be brought into God's family.

2. The strategy must fulfill that vision.

3. The church must eliminate all activities that do not lead to the goal.

Sadly, even churches that have a clear, stated vision often engage in many activities that have little or no relationship to achieving their vision. In a world of limited time and resources, no church can afford to waste time doing "good" things that are peripheral to its God-given purpose. The traditional church expends much energy on programs that have become self-perpetuating because that's the way it has always been done before, or because people in power positions have become untouchable. We must dare to stop maintaining traditions for their own sake and drop all baggage that does not help us fulfill our vision. This frees us to focus on our call, and to equip and mobilize every member to share in the strategy.

DEVELOPING THE VISION AND STRATEGY

In the early days of Faith Community Baptist Church, I learned an important lesson from Pastor Bill Yaegar of the First Baptist Church of Modesto, California. He affirmed that for any church to function well, it must have a vision—a corporate sense of where it is going and where it would like to be ten or fifteen years down the road. But Pastor Yaegar also taught me that a common vision is not enough to cause people to work and minister together. We must also have a common strategy in order to move in unity.

If my staff and I agreed that the Lord wanted us all to gather in

Kuala Lumpur next Monday, we would have a common vision. We would be equally committed to the idea of assembling in that capital city of Malaysia, up the peninsula from Singapore. But some of us might choose to fly there, others would go by car, while still others prefer to take the train—or even walk! Because there are different methods of obtaining the same goal, we would not be able to go together unless we agreed on the means.

Under the common vision of world evangelization, the Lord is now stirring up global strategies that are uniting many in the church to reach this goal. These strategies include prayer evangelism, strategic-level intercession, adopting hidden people groups, and the cell church model. Believers united under a common strategy find that they produce tremendous fruit as they work together in synergy.

Once a church has developed its own corporate vision and strategy, it needs to translate this into a program and plans, and then into tasks for carrying out the plans. The church, then, has four levels of responsibility: (1) vision, (2) strategy, (3) program/plans, and (4) tasks.

As leader of my church, I function on the first two levels differently from how I function on the last two. Because both vision and strategy must be shared among the body, I alone cannot make final decisions on these matters. The entire church, from the leadership team down, must have a common sense of ownership in the vision and strategy in order for the body to move together. In these matters I serve as a champion, a facilitator, an advocate of the vision and strategy. I articulate and refine the vision, rallying and persuading so that others not only catch the vision but make it their own.

Once the vision and strategy have been accepted and agreed on, however, I function as a chief executive officer, or commander, on the levels of program and task. I listen and receive input from others, then make the final decision. In this way the church advances together as an army under one banner.

This structure places me, as senior pastor, accountable to the church for two things: (1) Whatever program or task the church engages in must support the corporate vision and/or strategy. (2) Every year I must bring the church nearer to the vision. Within this perimeter, I have a free hand to lead as the Lord directs me. As the years go by, people at Faith Community Baptist Church have developed greater faith in my leadership as they see how I am moving the church toward our vision. When the church is aligned in the power of unity, the senior pastor enjoys a release of authority and freedom to follow the Lord's leading.

THE VISION AND STRATEGY OF FCBC

People have often asked how the vision of Faith Community Baptist Church came into being. I would like to say that I fasted 40 days, met with God on a mountaintop, and received the full revelation chiseled word for word on tablets of stone. The real story, however, is much less dramatic.

During the first year of FCBC, I had the leaders of the church join me in seeking the Lord for a clear vision and strategy for growth. We were determined not to be another church that religiously maintained traditional programs. With all our hearts, we sought the Lord for a blueprint that would enable us to take our city for God. The Lord showed us that to do this, we must move in unity, we must share a common vision, and we must agree on the appropriate strategies to fulfill the vision.

I personally spent much time before the Lord, asking where He wanted the church to be in ten or fifteen years. In response, I heard Him say to me, "What do *you* want for the church? If you could dream anything, what would you like? Go ahead, and I will bless it."

Over the years I have found that the Lord often gives me this kind of freedom. Sixteen hundred years ago, Augustine of Hippo said, "Love God and do what you like." If our hearts' greatest desire is to please the Lord we love, then the dreams in our hearts will be His.

I began to write down my dreams for the church. I sensed God saying He would give to me according to my faith. And since that season in early 1987, the Lord has enlarged both my faith and my vision.

Many Christians struggle with the notion of setting goals above what we can see or expect to be accomplished. We are afraid to dream big because we fear crossing the line into reckless presumption. The fact is that most of us have a faith level far below recklessness. We could stretch our faith way beyond our comfort zone and still not approach the edge of imprudence. As my friend Ed Silvoso, founder of Harvest Evangelism, says, "I would rather aim for a star and fall short than aim for a skunk and hit it."

It is important to write down the vision and strategy, to concretize them. Habakkuk 2:2 says, "Then the LORD answered me and said: 'Write the vision and make it plain on tablets, that he may run who reads it'" (NKJV). A vision not written down will not happen, because the leadership will find it difficult to keep the church motivated without clear goals. In addition, the inclusion of specific target dates makes the vision measurable. The vision can always be revised when the church is ready to grow beyond it.

Three-Part Vision

In early 1987, I and my leadership team developed a three-part vision that has guided our programs ever since. This three-part vision has seen refinements through the years. Today, it stands as follows:

By God's grace, we will, by the year 2001, (1) establish integrated ministries of outreach, discipleship, and service that encompass the whole of Singapore; (2) be a model cell group church that provides quality pastoral training and equipping resources for transitioning cell group churches in Singapore and around the world; and (3) establish 50 cell group churches around the world by sending out teams of at least three persons to reach unreached or responsive people groups.

Regarding part 1: Even before FCBC learned about cell church concepts from Dr. Ralph Neighbour, the Lord had given me a vision for a comprehensive network of both small groups and social services that touched the community. When Ralph presented us with the cell church model toward the end of 1987, I realized, "This is it! I see it! This is the strategy that will enable us to accomplish our vision."

Regarding part 2: Until a couple of years ago, this statement read "...in Singapore and Southeast Asia." The Lord has now expanded our vision to the world. I felt strongly that we needed to establish our own training program so that pastors could receive an impartation of leadership. Seminary professors with a gift of teaching can impart knowledge, but to learn to be a leader one must follow a person who is actually leading.

Regarding part 3: As of 1999, FCBC had planted only a handful of cell group churches in other people groups, toward our goal of 50 by the end of the year 2000. But we continue striving in pursuit of our God-given vision. By faith we believe that the training school we have established in Kazakhstan will produce a stream of missionaries planting churches throughout Asia and beyond. Already God is raising up indigenous believers from our cell church in Mongolia to go forth as church planters.

Ten Strategies

To achieve our three-part vision, we have adopted the following strategies, which continue to be refined:

1. Develop an exciting and meaningful celebration every weekend through music and the pulpit ministry.
2. Minimize committee meetings by decentralization of operations to full-time staff.

3. Commit to active staff recruitment to establish a multiple-staff ministry.
4. Establish a discipleship network for evangelism, prayer, and Bible study.
5. Provide lay leadership training for all leaders of the church.
6. Develop and establish specialized ministries of outreach.
7. Train, equip, send, and fully support missionaries from the church to the mission field.
8. Build a "Touch Center" consisting of an auditorium seating some 3,000, including other ministry facilities for both the church and the community.
9. Develop within every member a deep commitment to regular, disciplined, and intensive warfare prayer for spiritual revival in Singapore and around the world.
10. Strengthen the family so as to provide a solid base for reaching the unsaved with the love of Christ.

From the beginning, we were filled with a sense of excitement that God was going to fulfill these visions among us. In Faith Community Baptist Church, every one of us is given a corporate challenge to fulfill the vision the Lord has given. We believe that "everybody's job" becomes "nobody's job." Members of FCBC have pledged that, even if no one else will do it, we will assume the responsibility of winning our nation to the Lord. Before long, most of us began to realize that we could no longer possess this vision. Rather, this vision has now totally possessed us with a consuming zeal from the Lord!

THE GROWTH OF A UNITED VISION

The seeds of a new vision for a united ministry of the body in Singapore were planted in late 1993. By invitation of Dr. C. Peter Wagner, now president of the World Prayer Center in Colorado Springs,

I attended the first gathering of the International Spiritual Warfare Network in Seoul, Korea, in October 1993. Limited to 300 invitees, the meeting was dubbed "Gideon's Army." I came as a learner with little experience. During that week I observed and heard intercessors in action, saying and doing things I had never witnessed before. Two important lessons went home with me from that trip: (1) Unity of the body is necessary before revival can come and cities can be transformed. (2) Unity grows through identificational repentance and reconciliation.

Following this meeting, Peter Wagner asked me to provide leadership for the Spiritual Warfare Network in Singapore. This request stretched me. Back in 1986, I had been bad-mouthed as a pastor who split a church. In my hurt I had spent most of my time away from other Christian leaders, building FCBC. I felt I did not have the diplomacy to rally pastors from other churches.

The Lord, however, had a different perspective. I sensed Him telling me, "If you want to see your vision for your own church fulfilled, you must stand up and contribute to the unity of the body." So I took the coordinator position initially with a selfish motivation, and God then brought me beyond that.

At our first meeting, pastors got together simply to pray for one another personally, to work on relationships and get to know each other on a deeper level. Our friendships began to grow.

Then in June 1994, the global Day to Change the World, organized by Peter Wagner's United Prayer Track of the AD2000 & Beyond Movement, provided opportunity for people of different church backgrounds to come together and pray. In those early days, the open meetings consisted primarily of my own pastors and FCBC members— but we were beginning to mingle with the larger body of Christ in Singapore.

In 1995, Ed Silvoso's book *That None Should Perish* made an indelible impression on my heart. God soon birthed in me a new vision, one that would unite the church of our nation—Vision 2001, now known as Love Singapore. That year we held our first Singapore pastors' prayer summit, spending four days waiting on God with no agenda of our own. We prayed for each other, repented of sin, worshiped the Lord, and let Him speak to our hearts. On the final day, I shared what I had received about Vision 2001. Although the vision's huge scale felt rather scary, the other pastors agreed it came from God.

LOVE SINGAPORE

The Love Singapore vision looks toward the day when Singapore will become a city of worship, prayer, and mission under the banner of Christ. It is a strategy to light the darkness in our nation and beyond. The vision has five goals:

1. Unite the body.
2. Serve the community.
3. Establish a prayer cell in every housing block by 2000.
4. Launch a seven-wave harvest in 2001.
5. Every church to adopt an unreached people group.

As the annual pastors' prayer summit grew from 92 participants to 684 in the year 2000, God knitted us together like never before. Reconciliation took place between pastors and intercessors. The apostolic and the prophetic ministries began to function hand in hand. We underwent mass deliverance prayer. By now our relationships have gone beyond unity around a common vision. Today we feel bonded together in love and commitment to one another personally.

To pursue the goals of Love Singapore, we wanted to hold a March for Jesus in the downtown area, but knew we would never receive a governmental permit for such an event. So in 1996 TOUCH Community Services—a charitable organization started by FCBC that is staffed by professionals and supported by Christian volunteers—asked for and obtained permission to organize a benefit walkathon. Volunteers solicited pledges of money for the miles they would walk. Because we expected 6,000 participants, we requested an area to assemble and a stage so we could provide "warm-up" music and an encouraging speech before the volunteers set out. In this manner we held public worship, and then prayed for the city as we walked the route, using cards with suggested prayer points.

A year later other churches joined us, with 10,000 believers raising funds for TCS. Then in 1998, after the Asian financial crisis began, we established the Love Singapore Fund as an umbrella charity. This fund, which serves the community and ministers to the needy in the name of Jesus Christ, is not centrally controlled. Each participating church administers a share of the Love Singapore Fund on its own, under the common name.

At the 1998 walkathon, all the churches in Love Singapore came together. Some 40,000 people gathered on a large plot of reclaimed land across the harbor from the Central Business District to exalt Jesus together before heading out. As believers walked through downtown interceding for their country, I believe the church for the first time saw itself in all the beauty and power and potential it possesses in Christ. Moreover, charitable donations of one million Singaporean dollars flowed into the Love Singapore Fund! For the first time the media took note of how the Christian churches, in raising this money, showed their love for their country.

In both 1998 and 1999, the walkathon was preceded by a "cell light-up" event, when thousands of cell groups from churches all over Singapore prayed blessing on their neighborhoods. Other Christian leaders and I used a radio station in Batam, a nearby Indonesian island, to broadcast a coordinated agenda of prayer to each home hosting a cell meeting that night.

On the 1st of May 1999, more then 50,000 Christians gathered under predawn overcast skies for the "Taking the City Walk." We worshiped the Lord together, lifting up His name. Then believers stepped off on two different routes that converged at the end, surrounding the Central Business District. The body of Christ surpassed the previous year's fundraising record while interceding for the advance of God's kingdom throughout Singapore.

The churches of our nation continue to press toward fulfillment of each of the five goals of Love Singapore. This vision has done more to unite the church of Jesus Christ in this country than any other movement in Singapore's history.

BIRTH PANGS OF NEW VISION

The Lord began birthing a new vision in my heart following a trip to Guatemala and Argentina in October/November 1998. I had been experiencing some tension with my pastoral team when my travel outside Singapore began to increase. The other pastors would sometimes ask me if a particular trip was going to facilitate Part 2 or Part 3 of our three-part vision. Some ministry trips didn't quite fit anywhere in the FCBC vision.

Then in Argentina, in November 1998, I heard a new word from God. "I have given you a ministry way beyond Faith Community Baptist Church," I sensed Him saying. "You can't position everything under the structure of the church, or its resources will be strained. You need to develop a ministry above FCBC—an apostolic ministry."

As I mulled over this word, I realized that the three-part vision may be fulfilled by FCBC, but that other visions, intended for elsewhere, may or may not involve the church. I also knew that FCBC was nearing the time to birth its own new vision, since our current one has been pegged to the year 2000.

This year I have wrestled through new birth pangs, including a sense of tension and inefficiency, as God is in the process of revealing new things and bringing them forth.

I know that two structures we have currently in place will provide key leadership for future ministry. One is WorldCells International (WCI), incorporated in the United States. This organization partners with churches in mission, rallying them around the goal of planting cell group churches around the world. The other is Touch Ministries International (TMI), which helps traditional churches transition to the cell model.

Now I believe the Lord is asking me to start a new humanitarian foundation, a worldwide charitable ministry that transcends Touch Community Services. I have a dream that this new Touch humanitarian foundation will become known around the world as widely as the Red Cross, that we will be first on the scene whenever a disaster takes place. Drawing from a combination of resources from different parts of the globe, the foundation will begin to transform communities and nations as they receive an overwhelming abundance of love and service in the name of Jesus Christ.

The Lord has also spoken to me about a Joseph ministry that will be able to mobilize and manage resources to bless entire nations. God is calling forth businesspeople, economists, humanitarians, development workers, education specialists, medical professionals— as well as apostles, prophets, and others—to join teams to go into such countries as Indonesia and present their leaders, in the name of Jesus, with a "turnkey solution" to national challenges. The vision of this ministry is to demonstrate the love and power of the gospel on national and governmental levels with no strings attached, through massive humanitarian and developmental programs as well as major participation in business activity.

We are now beginning to put together an investment holding company that could be owned by an apostolic council or by the church itself. Starting with seed money of US$10 million, we hope to raise this amount to $100 million. Through such means we will be able to create jobs and bring in a complete package to turn around struggling nations.

History shows that the gospel has often spread through economic trading. In our day, Muslims have their own well-known business syndicates that they use as stepping-stones to Islamize nations. Dare we, as the Christian church, fail to enlarge our vision to such levels? If there is truth in the adage, "Money talks," we should strategize ways to have money talk for Jesus.

Such a venture requires tremendous prayer covering because it will handle major megabucks. As part of the vision for a new apostolic network, these organizations will need a structure that provides both accountability and freedom.

WHAT IS YOUR VISION?

Perhaps some of these ideas will seem overwhelming to those just beginning to formulate a vision for a local church of 100 people. This is understandable. We should not compare the size of our vision to the size of someone else's vision. We should, however, compare our vision to the size of the task before us. Do we really believe that God can win our nation for Jesus Christ? Do we believe He wants to? Do we believe we each have a role in accomplishing this task? It may be easy to declare such a belief while cheering at a Christian rally, but hard to maintain it when we go out and look into the faces of thousands and millions of lost souls around us.

We cannot truly believe for what is humanly impossible until God births in us a vision. We need to have a dream for Jesus Christ. When the Spirit of God spreads the vision and unites the people of God, we will begin to say together, "This is the day of salvation for my land. This is the day when we will see the glory of God." I pray that as you seek the Lord for your part in what He is doing, He will expand your faith and burn a new vision within you that will cause you to rise up and fulfill His purposes in this generation.

Five

Reliance on the Holy Spirit:

— Power Source of the Cell Church —

"God has forgiven you. Are you willing to forgive yourself?"

The 16-year-old girl sitting across my office stared at me as I asked this question. Suddenly, her eyeballs rolled back and all I saw was the white of her eyes. Then out of this young girl came forth a deep masculine voice: *"I will not let her go."*

An eerie fear rose within me, and immediately I bowed in prayer. I was not praying for her. I was praying for myself! One thought filled my mind: "Lord, don't let this demon get near me!"

Eventually, I cast out the demon—out of my office, together with the teenager. "Sister, you need help. You should get yourself a psychiatrist," were my last words to her.

Susan (not her real name) had been coming to me for prayer over her depression. She suffered from insomnia and lapsed repeatedly into a despondency that immobilized her. I discovered that she had had an affair with a married man. As a church-going Christian, she was ridden with guilt. In the process of the counseling I gave her, she followed all my recommendations: She broke up with the man, asked forgiveness from the Lord and her parents, and sought to walk with the Lord through Bible reading and prayer. Still, she could not shake loose the heavy burden of guilt and despair.

I asked her to memorize and recite 1 John 1:9 over and over: "If we confess our sins, he is faithful and just and will forgive us our sins and purify us from all unrighteousness." She did so. Yet this did not set her free from her bondage.

Then I had the insight about her need to forgive herself. That's when the demon manifested. Pathetically, I sent the teenager away, not knowing what else to do.

Susan walked into my office five or six weeks later, filled with the joy of the Lord. She had been completely set free from depression and was now sleeping peacefully. "How did it happen?" I asked her, eager to learn how to deal with the same problem in the future. "Did you see the psychiatrist?"

"No, Pastor," she replied. Somewhat hesitantly, she reported that she had attended a healing service at a small charismatic church. The power of God came upon her and completely delivered her from the demon that had plagued her with depression.

I was flabbergasted. *What do they have that I don't have?* I wondered. Here I was, a graduate of Dallas Theological Seminary with a master's degree in theology. I served as senior pastor of the largest and fastest-growing Southern Baptist church in Singapore. Well known for my solidly biblical, theologically astute, yet down-to-earth and heart-stirring expository messages each Sunday, I had seen my church grow from 300 to 1,600 within five years. Yet this incident wakened me with a shock to my spiritual impotence. Four years of seminary training never taught me how to deal with a 16-year-old girl who speaks in a man's voice. My heart began to thirst for a deeper experience of God. I cried out to Him, "Lord, I need to know you more. I need more of you and more of your power!"

The Lord loves to answer this kind of prayer. Jesus said, "If anyone is thirsty, let him come to me and drink. Whoever believes in me, as the Scripture has said, streams of living water will flow from within him" (John 7:37–38).

DRINK OF HIS POWER

As I hungered for the Lord and His power, I began an exciting journey of coming to know intimately the most powerful personality on earth—the Holy Spirit. I had known Him in my mind theologically as the third person of the Godhead. I had understood that He lives within me. Yet, like many other believers, I had not really known Him in an intimate way through my own experience.

According to A. W. Tozer, the well-respected evangelical pastor and author, the Holy Spirit is the most neglected person of the Godhead. In his book *The Divine Conquest,* Tozer writes:

> In neglecting or denying the deity of Christ the Liberals have committed a tragic blunder, for it leaves them nothing but an imperfect Christ whose death was a mere martyrdom and whose resurrection is a myth. They who follow a merely human Saviour follow no Saviour at all, but an ideal only, and one furthermore that can do no more than mock their weaknesses and sins....

> But however culpable the act of the Liberal in denying the Godhood of Christ, we who pride ourselves on our orthodoxy must not allow our indignation to blind us to our own shortcomings. Certainly this is no time for self-congratulations, for we too have in recent years committed a costly blunder in religion, a blunder paralleling closely that of the Liberal. Our blunder (or shall we frankly say our sin?) has been to neglect the doctrine of the Spirit to a point where we virtually deny Him His place in the Godhead. This denial has not been by open doctrinal statement, for we have clung closely enough to the Biblical position wherever our credal pronouncements are concerned. Our formal creed is sound; *the breakdown is in our working creed....*

Our neglect of the doctrine of the blessed Third Person has had and is having serious consequences....The doctrine of the Spirit is buried dynamite. Its power awaits discovery and use by the Church. The power of the Spirit will not be given to any mincing assent to pneumatological truth. The Holy Spirit cares not at all whether we write Him into our credenda in the back of our hymnals; He waits for our *emphasis*....When the Holy Spirit ceases to be incidental and again becomes fundamental the power of the Spirit will be asserted once more among the people called Christians. (pp. 64–66, emphasis original)

How descriptive these words are of my own Christian pilgrimage! My theology and understanding of the Holy Spirit seemed so soundly biblical. Yet I realized how little I really knew Him and how much I lacked experience of His person, His ways, and His power.

This condition describes many in the church today. Solid biblical theology masks an experience of the Holy Spirit that is spiritually bankrupt. In our ignorance, we neglect Him and even fear Him when He works in ways unfamiliar to us. Through my own pilgrimage, however, I have become convinced that reliance on the Holy Spirit is a prerequisite for successful transition to and functioning of the cell church.

There are three truths concerning the Holy Spirit that many evangelical Christians believe in their minds but do not really accept in their hearts. Although they confess these truths in words, they deny them in daily living and ministry.

1. The Holy Spirit is a Person.

First of all, the Holy Spirit is a person. He is not a thing, not an impersonal force, not an influence, but a living person. Now, I don't have to go through all the theological arguments showing that the

Holy Spirit is a person. Any standard book on systematic theology will do an adequate job defending this truth. My point is that many of us cannot really relate to the Holy Spirit as a person.

Most Christians have no trouble thinking of God the Father as a person. We all have had human fathers and know something about that kind of relationship. We think of the Father speaking to the Israelites from Mount Sinai in the Old Testament. He delivered the people from Egypt. He was the Almighty One who led them into the Promised Land. When we talk to God the Father, we have little problem conceiving of Him as a person with intellect, emotion, and will. God the Father is someone who can think, feel, and assert His will. We can relate to that.

And, of course, thinking of God the Son, Jesus Christ, as a person is even easier. We can picture Him as a person relating to us, because He lived on earth in a human body. We have no trouble going to the Lord Jesus and saying, "O Jesus, I love you. I need you."

However, when we come to the Holy Spirit, the third person in the Godhead, we often do not know what to make of Him. Part of our difficulty comes from the various metaphors the Bible uses to describe His ministry. We wonder—is He a wind? Is He a dove? Is He oil? Is He fire? Is He a cloud? Many of us, when we think about the Holy Spirit, have a mental image of some inanimate object, or simply a force or power. It is pretty hard for us to relate personally to wind or oil or fire or even a dove. How do we say to the wind, "Hi, how are you?" Or to the fire, "I love you, fire!" Or "Thank you, oil, for your anointing upon me."

I remember when I first sung that simple chorus most of us know today: "Father, I love you, I praise you, I adore you. Glorify your name in all the earth." Singing the first stanza to the Father was natural. The second stanza posed no problem either. With deep conviction I freely sang, "Jesus, I love you, I praise you, I adore you. Glorify your name in all the earth." But when I came to the third stanza as I sang it for the first time, my mind bent into knots. "Spirit, I love you? I praise you? I adore you? Glorify your name?" A sense of uneasiness crept over me. Yes, I understood theologically that the Holy Spirit is a person. Yet I had never quite related to Him as a living personality.

The Bible indicates that the Holy Spirit has intellect, emotion, and will, just as the other persons of the Godhead. Romans 8:27 refers to "the mind of the Spirit." Likewise, the Holy Spirit must have emotion, because we can grieve Him (Ephesians 4:30). He makes rational decisions, because 1 Corinthians 12:11 (NAS) says that the Spirit distributes His gifts "to each one individually just as He wills."

The apostle Paul closes his letter of 2 Corinthians with this benediction: "May the grace of the Lord Jesus Christ, and the love of God, and the fellowship of the Holy Spirit be with you all" (13:14). For years the body of Christ has received freely from the grace of the Lord Jesus. We have drunk deeply of the love of God. Now it is time to draw near to the person of the Holy Spirit and enjoy true fellowship with Him.

2. The Holy Spirit is God.

No Bible-believing Christian would deny that the Holy Spirit is God. Most of us can articulate the doctrine of the Trinity, one God in three persons. The Scripture is clear. Deuteronomy 6:4 states, "Hear, O Israel: The LORD our God, the LORD is one." God is one in essence. Yet He is three in person. It is a mystery, but we believe it.

The doctrine of the Trinity means that God the Father is fully God. He is neither one-third God, nor one-third part of God. The same is true of God the Son, Jesus Christ. And—yes—the same is true of the Holy Spirit. Each is fully God and the fullness of God at the same time. We believe this as part of our doctrine. Deep in the recesses of our hearts and spirits, however, many of us have relegated the Holy Spirit to someone who is less than fully God.

I have found myself together with many of my fellow ministers of the gospel making a statement that in effect denies the full deity of the Holy Spirit in our lives and practice. For years I warned my church, "Now as for Holy Spirit, let's be balanced in our thinking. Be careful not to go overboard on this subject. We must be sure that we do not overemphasize the Holy Spirit."

Have you heard this one before? Or have you actually made the same statement, as I have? If so, we need to repent of this sinful confession. Think about it: "Do not overemphasize the Holy Spirit." This statement relegates the third person of the Godhead to a lesser position. Have we ever told anyone, "Be careful not to overemphasize God the Father"? Or "Be careful not to overemphasize Jesus Christ"? Absolutely not! We will never say such a thing because we know that the Father is God and the Son is God. God can never be overemphasized. Yet many of us have the audacity to say, "Be careful not to overemphasize the Holy Spirit." We do so because deep within our spirits, we do not really think of Him as fully God. Here lies the difference between our credal confession and our actual conviction.

During my pastorate at my former church, I entered a season of growth in my sensitivity to the ministry of the Holy Spirit in my life. I remember mentioning this in one of my Sunday sermons. I shared with the congregation how I had learned to speak to the Holy Spirit on an intimate level. Whenever I counseled a person with an emotional problem, for instance, I would say, "Holy Spirit, please help me to know what is going on in this person's life." Or if I did not feel freedom in my heart to preach when I stood behind the pulpit, I would quietly talk to the Holy Spirit: "Holy Spirit, what is wrong here, Lord?" Or when I preached a great sermon and people responded to the Word of the Lord, I would say, "Holy Spirit, you are doing a great job here!"

A deacon met me at the church office the following week. He told me I had made a serious error in my previous week's sermon.

"Pastor," he said as politely as he could, "it is theologically not right for us to pray to the Holy Spirit. We should pray only to God the Father, in the name of Jesus, and by the power of the Spirit." (Wow! This sounds like a classic line right out of a textbook on systematic theology!)

I happened to have a Baptist hymnal with me in the office. I turned to a familiar hymn, "Spirit of the Living God, Fall Fresh on Me." I said to my brother, "Please tell me if this hymn is a hymn of prayer."

"No doubt about it," he replied.

"To whom is this prayer directed?" I continued.

Sheepishly he responded, "To the Holy Spirit."

I then went through the hymnal with him. Every single hymn regarding the Holy Spirit was a prayer directed to the Holy Spirit. Why is it that we don't have a problem praying to the Lord Jesus, even when the Scripture does not have explicit instruction that we should direct our prayers to Him? The answer is simple. We are convinced that the Lord Jesus is truly God. We have no problem calling upon His name in prayer. Yet, tragically, at the deepest level of our heart, we lack complete conviction that the Holy Spirit is fully God.

God has compassion for those in ignorance. But when revelation exposes our unbelief, we must repent or face His judgment. It is time to turn away from mindsets and practices that neglect the Holy Spirit and relegate Him to a lesser form of divinity.

3. The Holy Spirit is God in the Now!

The Holy Spirit is not only a person, He is not only God, but He is God in the *now*. The third person of the Godhead is the one who manifests the reality of God in our daily lives. He is the "Paraclete," the one who comes alongside us to counsel and guide us. He comforts us. He leads us into all truth (John 16:13), which means that the

Holy Spirit takes the truths of God and makes them real in our lives. The Holy Spirit demonstrates the power of God through signs and wonders. Jesus Himself performed His miracles by the power of the Holy Spirit in order to manifest the presence of God among the people (Acts 10:38). The gifts of the Holy Spirit in the church demonstrate the manifested presence of God among His people (1 Corinthians 14:25). Indeed, He is God in the *now!*

The reason most of us tend to neglect the Holy Spirit is that we don't really expect God to show up right here, right now. We are so engrossed doing our religious thing week after week that we don't expect to see or experience the manifested presence of God in our midst. This is why, when God does show up in some churches, people get disturbed, because His visitation upsets our familiar routine. I know well how this works, because this was my pattern for many years.

While I always had a heart for God and believed that He wanted to use me, when I prayed for Him to do so I didn't fully know what I was asking for. I had both gifting and training to preach, and God used me effectively that way. He still does. As time went on my church grew and I preached to more and more people. But God began opening my eyes to see that, while preaching can change lives, something was missing.

One Sunday I did something I had never done before. I invited people with sin in their lives to come to the altar and confess. Long-time church members, people I had thought of as spiritual, confessed sins of immorality, homosexuality, and all kinds of evil.

I was astonished. "I have been preaching God's Word on all these issues," I brooded. "How could the message have failed to have an impact on so many people?" I began to realize there were situations beyond my ability to help, despite all my Bible knowledge. I lacked faith to expect supernatural power in my ministry. In short, I needed to experience the Holy Spirit as God in the now.

ARE THE HOLY SPIRIT'S GIFTS FOR TODAY?

I graduated from a seminary in the United States that taught me for four years that the supernatural gifts of the Holy Spirit, including tongues, healing, miracles, prophecy, and so on, ceased at the end of the apostolic age. When I first returned to Singapore to become pastor of the Southern Baptist church in which I grew up, Pastor David Yonggi Cho of Korea was holding healing services at the biggest sports stadium in Singapore. I was asked to give the position of my church with regard to these meetings. For nine Sundays I spoke on the subject of the work and gifts of the Holy Spirit. In my ignorance and arrogance, I thought I presented a watertight case showing that what Pastor Cho was doing was unbiblical and perhaps even heretical. I actually enjoyed tearing to pieces the theology of those in the charismatic camp.

Slowly the Lord began to challenge my thinking. Although the church grew under my leadership, I could see that I lacked power to deal with situations beyond my control, and therefore could not convey such power to any of my church members. After my failure to help the demonized girl whose story I told at the beginning of this chapter, both discouragement and spiritual hunger put a restlessness in my soul. Where was the God of the Bible in my own life? I wanted to be like the apostle Paul, but where was the God of Paul?

When I prayed for the sick in the hospital, I rarely saw any change in condition because I didn't really expect God to heal. Especially for people suffering serious or terminal illnesses, my feeble prayers reflected an attitude of defeat. "O God, please give him peace! Give his wife and children peace!" Because I held no hope for recovery, I could only pray that the patient would die in peace and that God would comfort the family.

The Lord began to challenge my heart about the issue of the cessation of spiritual gifts. Although I knew all the scriptural arguments backwards and forwards to show that the supernatural gifts of the

Spirit were not for today, God provoked me to wrestle through this issue. When the demonized girl I had counseled received complete deliverance and healing at the charismatic church, I could not deny what had happened. Her real-life testimony forced me to reconsider the truth of what I had been taught.

This process of paradigm shift stretched me in painful ways. I had to put my reputation on the line. But I found God very gracious. I had sincerely believed my former position. It was the only way I had been taught. When God began to reveal the truth to me, however, I had a choice: to become entrenched in my belief, or to admit I had been wrong. I got on my knees and repented of this doctrine. "Lord, I've sinned against you," I confessed. "I have taught something wrong. Please forgive me."

Now I had a problem. Having acknowledged that all the gifts of the Spirit still exist today, I could not with integrity continue to minister in the same old way. But how in the world could I encourage the exercise of gifts I had never seen or experienced? I had never attended a charismatic service in my life because I was so sure that contemporary tongues came from either the flesh or the devil. How could I stir up these gifts?

I sensed the Lord telling me, "The first thing you need to do is to start praying for the sick." He showed me that gifts surface in churches that encourage and exercise those gifts. Traditional churches, for instance, will often raise up plenty of people with teaching gifts and few or none with healing gifts, matching the pattern of gifts exercised in those churches.

My church services already allowed a brief time for people to come to the kneelers in front and seek God in silence. I determined to use that time to pray for the sick also. I announced to the congregation, "The Bible says in James 5 that if anyone is sick, he should call the elders to pray and anoint him with oil. Many of you may think you would have to be on the verge of dying before doing that, but why wait that long? If you are sick, call upon the elders. I have with me this bottle of olive oil."

I had never done this before nor seen it done, and no one had taught me how to do it. But I wanted to obey the Lord. One time I emptied a whole bottle of oil on someone's head! Despite my mistakes, God began to work. Nothing dramatic—no dead people raised. I preferred to start with coughs, colds, headaches, and the like. As testimonies of healing accumulated, however, my faith level increased—and with it my hunger for more.

"FILL ME WITH THE HOLY SPIRIT"

Someone gave me a very dangerous book called *Nine O'Clock in the Morning* by Dennis Bennett. My theological grid became even more confused. I didn't know what to think about the so-called baptism of the Holy Spirit. One day I was so mentally exhausted I cried out in prayer, "God, I just want to know what this is! I want to get a touch from you."

At that time I had been invited to speak at an evangelistic meeting in Brunei. Because Brunei is a strict Muslim country, only about 40 people attended the meeting, with just three or four of them unbelievers. I had told the organizers that I wanted to fast and pray during my visit, preaching in the evenings and spending the days praying in my room.

During those few days, I prayed and cried and waited upon the Lord. The more I read the Bible, the more confused I became. Finally I prayed, "Lord, I don't know what this gift of the Spirit is, but please just give it to me!" Soon afterwards, a new faith rose in my heart. I remembered reading a book that suggested tongues involved just moving out in faith. I determined to try. "Lord, fill me with the Holy Spirit," I prayed.

How do you begin to speak a language you don't understand? I started out with a song. I opened my mouth and sang, "Something beautiful, something good...." The rest of the song came out in unknown syllables. I stopped to check myself by declaring, "Jesus is Lord and He came in the flesh." The fear of demonic influence still lingered! Then I continued speaking in the new language, repeating this declaration periodically several more times.

Frankly, however, this experience disappointed me. It was quite rational and unemotional. I thought being filled with the Spirit meant shouting and screaming, jumping up and down. Only later did I realize the scripture in 1 Corinthians 14:4 says, "He who speaks in a tongue edifies himself," not "He who speaks in a tongue feels good." I learned that this kind of sign engages not primarily emotion (a component of the soul) but the spirit.

I also had supposed perhaps God would overcome me. Sometimes He does this, but normally only demons like to force themselves on people. Most miracles involve 100 percent God and 100 percent human vessel. When Peter walked on water, for instance, God could not have performed the miracle unless Peter got out of the boat.

Immediately afterwards, I noticed a great freedom in my preaching. At previous evangelistic meetings, I always felt pressure to see new converts raise their hands. But that week in Brunei, I felt carefree. I told the people, "If Lawrence Khong speaks, you can make your own decision. But if the Holy Spirit speaks, you ain't got a chance!"

It was true. Although only three or four unbelievers attended the meetings, every one of them became a Christian. In fact, they came forward at the invitation every time I preached. The Lord was affirming me.

PAYING THE PRICE FOR MORE OF GOD

After I returned home to Singapore, I was preparing my sermon for the next Sunday when I suddenly saw a mental picture of myself at the pulpit. I saw many hands raised and people coming forward to receive Christ. In those days I didn't give an invitation every week, and I hadn't announced in advance that this would be a "gospel Sunday" when people should bring their unsaved friends. But my faith rose to believe what God was showing me.

I called my staff and asked them to prepare counselors to stand by and assist those who would trust Christ that week. On a typical "gospel Sunday," we might have about three new converts. My staff wanted to have faith so they prepared ten counselors.

That Sunday, 30 people raised their hands at the invitation. All the counselors had to double up. I heard the Lord say to me, "I've just touched your heart, and I am doing a new work in you."

Now I understand why God often uses tongues to release us into other gifts of the Spirit. Although it is not the only sign of the fullness of the Spirit, it is a common one in Scripture, as well as a gateway to other gifts. For so many of us, the confines of our intellectual understanding prevent us from doing anything we cannot explain. When I first spoke in my new language, I felt stupid. But in humbling myself to do so, I overcame the bondage of my intellect and its limitations. I submitted my mind to the Lord and let God be God. I gave Him the freedom to speak.

God then began to open me to the new world of the Spirit. And, as I have told the story before, I got fired from my church.

I had to pay a price for teaching wrong doctrines in the past, as well as for choosing to do what was right once God challenged and convicted me. The Lord began releasing me from the fear of man.

Spiritual gifts, or *charismata* in New Testament Greek, are just that—gifts. We do not earn them through study or spirituality or holiness. They do not come as rewards for maturity. They do not identify leaders or those with spiritual offices. The gifts of the Spirit come as free favors of God's love and grace. The only prerequisite is that we have the Holy Spirit living in us, through Christ, and allow ourselves to be used by God in whatever way He desires.

THE VISITATIONS OF THE SPIRIT

One of the reasons Faith Community Baptist Church has successfully managed the transition to a cell church has to do with the visitations of the Spirit. The Holy Spirit has visited our church a number of times. Let me tell you about two powerful occasions.

In 1991 we sponsored John Wimber and a team of his pastors from the Vineyard Christian Fellowship to come to Singapore. I was not yet very sensitive to the Spirit. I enjoyed the seminars but did not sense any particularly powerful presence or anointing. On the day I took John back to the airport, he asked me, "What did you think of last night?"

"It was OK," I said.

"Lawrence," John replied, "that was about the greatest manifestation of God you could ever experience on earth up to this point!"

Shock and disappointment gripped me. "That was the greatest manifestation? I didn't feel a thing!"

But God wasn't through yet. On Sunday when I preached a message on repentance, people flocked to come forward. I had never seen so many respond. Not only that, everyone to my left side lay flat on the floor! No one had touched them.

This astounded me. Nothing similar had ever happened in my ministry. I always thought that people who fell were responding to psychological manipulation. That morning, however, the Lord took control. By the third of our four services, people coming in commented, "There's something unusual here today...," and before they could finish their sentence they slumped to the floor.

This kind of manifestation is not new. During Solomon's dedication of the Temple in 1 Kings 8:11, the glory of the Lord came and rested there so powerfully that the priests could not stand. The same presence and glory can visit us today. The Holy Spirit is God in the now!

This visitation sparked a six-month season of deep repentance among members of the church. No matter what I preached on, people came forward in tears to confess and repent of all kinds of sins. Moreover, no one expressed reluctance to join a cell group. The general attitude of the church said, "The Lord is here, Pastor. I'll do whatever you say!" The anointing of the Spirit filled the cell meetings. The sick were healed, and the demonized were set free. The church entered a season of tremendous growth as our cell groups learned to minister in the power of the Spirit.

Then in late 1994, the Lord visited us again. One Sunday when many of us felt spiritually dry, at the end of an hour-long prayer meeting I asked if anyone felt the presence of the Lord. I invited those who did to come forward. Spontaneously, people started laughing. A wave of joy hit the room. One woman with a normally serious personality began to laugh and dance before the Lord.

One man at the nine o'clock service stood up to come forward but fell under the power of the Spirit. He couldn't move until five o'clock in the afternoon. Through four services, people had to climb over him. In fact, we eventually ran out of floor space because fallen people lay all over the stage, unable to get up. Another man was actually rolling on the floor.

As I picked my way over bodies to get to the pulpit for the third service, God did something in my heart. Since then I have not been disturbed by crying children in the services. After all, if we let people laugh, why not let children cry?

For several weeks I preached through that move of God, and the Holy Spirit reached out to the cells as well. And I was greatly blessed to see my own brother's life touched.

My brother has a quiet personality, just the opposite of me. He had attended church with me for many years but never felt ready to receive baptism. He and his wife attended a cell group at the beginning of this new outpouring, and there the Lord gave his wife a blessing of laughter that lasted all night long. My brother couldn't believe what had happened to her. Neither one of them is a particularly emotional person. She then suggested that he check it out: "Why don't you go forward in church next week?"

Although somewhat skeptical, he did. The altar area was packed. When I saw him and came over, I touched him gently, saying, "God bless you." And down he went.

After that service, everyone lying on the stage got up except my brother. From the floor he heard me preach twice more that day! When I asked him about it later, he told me, "I didn't feel anything. All I know is that you prayed and the next moment I was on the floor. I thought someone had pushed me down. I immediately wanted to stand up but found myself immobilized. The only thing on my mind was getting up the minute I could do it."

Good fruit came out of this experience. In January 1995 my brother was baptized. By April he led someone to Christ in our church's spring harvest event. He has won new converts in each campaign since then, and now he leads a cell group.

RECEIVE THE HOLY SPIRIT

The structure of the cell church is nothing but a conduit for the power of the Holy Spirit. Unless the living water flows, our churches are dead, our cells are lifeless, and our lives are powerless. We must give space to the Holy Spirit to let Him be God in our midst. We cannot run our lives, our cells, or our churches without Him and expect to see lasting fruit.

The Bible encourages us to "test everything" (1 Thessalonians 5:21). Not all manifestations come from the Holy Spirit. In every move of God, some works of the flesh and the devil will be mixed in. But the same verse tells us to "hold on to the good." Don't be afraid to put up with some excesses while you discern what is of God. If you shut down everything right away, you could easily miss your time of visitation.

What does it take to receive the touch of the Holy Spirit? Let me suggest three things.

The first step is to thirst. Jesus invites us, "If anyone is thirsty, let him come to me and drink" (John 7:37). Recognize your need for deeper experience and intimacy with God. If you are feeling dry, hungry, and thirsty, Jesus wants to satisfy you with the Holy Spirit's river of living water. Thirst will compel you to press in and keep seeking everything God has for you.

The second step is to believe. To receive, just believe that God will give to you when you ask in the name of His Son, Jesus Christ. He promises that when we ask for bread He will not give us a stone. In fact, "...how much more will your Father in heaven give the Holy Spirit to those who ask him!" (Luke 11:13). Then step out in faith, without fear. Don't be passive about receiving God's gift. Be like Peter and get out of the boat to walk on water!

The third step is to drink. Drinking is easy. You don't have to study or prepare to drink. You just take the glass handed to you and swallow the water it holds. Receiving the Holy Spirit is not the time to get too serious. Enjoy God like a little child at play! He delights in you, and He invites you to experience more of Him than you ever have before. I guarantee that when you do, your life and your church will never be the same.

Six

ROARING
AS A LION:

The Role of the Senior Pastor
— in the Cell Church —

Pastors wear many hats. Their churches often expect them to juggle countless roles and responsibilities with the dexterity of a circus performer. One church even put out this classified ad: "Wanted: the perfect pastor. Approximately 28 years old, with 30 years' preaching experience. Must have a heart for the youth, work well with the elderly, participate in church sports, visit every hospitalized member. Need top-flight negotiation skills, good singing voice, and expertise in repair of office equipment, church van, and fellowship hall plumbing. Office hours 7 a.m. till 10 p.m. Salary $100 per week. Will preferably tithe $50 per week, wear fashionable suits, have a large library. Must participate in evangelism outreaches, make 30 calls per day on church members, always be in the office when parishioners phone. Walking on water a plus."

No wonder studies rate the pastorate as one of the most stressful occupations in the world! Yet pastors sometimes add to their stress by not understanding and keeping in balance different aspects of their leadership position that can help ease their load. A pastor can move into a more successful and satisfying ministry by maintaining a proper perspective on the multiple roles that come with the pastoral calling.

THREE ASPECTS OF PASTORAL MINISTRY

The Bible highlights three aspects of the pastoral ministry. These roles apply to all pastors, not just senior pastors, and to all churches, not just cell churches. They are shepherding, managing, and leading.

Shepherding

Shepherding is the most commonly understood aspect of the pastoral ministry. Indeed, the Greek word for pastor means shepherd. In 1 Peter 5:2, Peter advises his readers, "Be shepherds of God's flock that is under your care, serving as overseers...." Most of our seminary training prepares us to be shepherds, to teach and feed the flock, to love and care for the sheep.

Yet even the most gifted and talented shepherds—if shepherding is all they do—will not fulfill God's vision for their church. Why? A pastor with a heart for the sheep, who spends time nurturing and encouraging each one, quickly draws more people to the church. Soon the church grows so large that the pastor can no longer adequately minister to each member. People begin to mutter, "What's happened to our pastor? He never visits me any more." The good, loving shepherd becomes a victim of his own success.

Some pastors, in their warm devotion to people, have determined, "I will never let my church grow beyond my ability to know the name of each member." While such a shepherd's heart is admirable, a whole community of lost people needs the same kind of nurture. I can't imagine having the size of my church dependent on my memory!

Success and growth in pastoral ministry will require two other areas just as important as shepherding.

Managing

Some Christians think of management as a secular, unspiritual activity, unsuitable for church pastors. But the Bible commends it. Paul's advice regarding bishops and overseers in 1 Timothy 3:5 applies equally well to pastors and all church leaders: "If anyone does not know how to manage his own family, how can he take care of God's church?" Managing a home involves everything from keeping a budget to distributing chores to planning the family vacation. Running a church, especially a large church, requires even more management skill. A good pastor will be a good manager.

Churches open to the move of the Holy Spirit often have the most problems with this aspect of pastoral ministry. An emphasis on being Spirit-controlled should never keep us from proper order and management. The gifted but dysfunctional first-century Corinthian church shows the dangers of this trap! Many problems in churches arise not from spiritual issues but from management issues. If management problems are not dealt with, however, they will become spiritual problems. Demons can take advantage of poor management and make things worse.

The cell church structure is actually a management structure. Using this framework, a church can grow to unlimited size while maintaining excellent pastoral care for the sheep. Still, another aspect of ministry is needed.

Leading

Leadership is the most difficult aspect of the pastoral ministry. Even the secular business world struggles with the concept. Many authors have penned books trying to pin down the nature of leadership, how to become a good leader, and how to train others as good leaders. Some even question whether leaders can be trained, or whether they are born rather than made.

Hebrews 13:17 says, "Obey your leaders and submit to their authority. They keep watch over you as men who must give an account." If we grant that this verse should not provide license for a pastor to dominate a church, what does it mean to have authoritative leadership?

Leaders in the body of Christ are those who can rally the people of God around the purposes of God. The Holy Spirit anoints some men and women to rise up and lead others in paths of righteousness, obedience to God, and passion for the lost. Captured by a vision from the Lord, a leader can stand and declare to others what God is saying, and they will listen and follow. The difference between managing and leading could be summarized this way: Management is doing things right, while leadership is doing right things—in the right time and the right way.

One of the greatest needs of the church of Jesus Christ is leadership. Unless God raises up strong individuals without self-interest who can hear from the Lord, receive His direction, and lead the body in His purposes, the devil will raise up others for his own purposes.

All three aspects of the pastoral ministry—shepherding, managing, and leading—must operate in strength in order to have a growing, effective church.

SHEPHERDING, MANAGING, AND LEADING AT ALL LEVELS

In a cell church, all levels of leadership—from the cell group leader to the senior pastor—will exercise these three aspects of ministry in different proportions. Leaders at the cell level provide the bulk of pastoral care through their shepherding responsibilities. Zone supervisors and zone pastors add more management functions. The district pastor's primary role is to manage, while the senior pastor focuses mostly on leading. But all levels of leadership need the full scope of skills and anointing to shepherd, manage, and lead those in their care.

For instance, more and better shepherding takes place at the cell group level when the cell leader, exercising management skills, delegates some administrative responsibilities to others. Good cell leaders train their cell interns in all aspects of cell group ministry.

And the most vibrantly growing cells are those led by men or women with leadership ability who hear the Lord's direction for their cell and communicate that vision.

These three aspects of ministry—shepherding, managing, and leading—illustrate three aspects of the nature of the church that must also be kept in balance. The church is a community, a corporation, and a cause.

Community, Corporation, and Cause

In a community, where shepherding predominates, the people involved see each other as brothers and sisters in a family. In a corporation, built on management, people relate to each other as workers in a business. In a cause, leadership is most important, and people interact in a way similar to soldiers in a military environment.

In a community, people matter most of all. In a corporation, process matters. In a cause, purpose matters. The shepherds of a community provide strength and build trust. The managers of a corporation provide structure and empower people. The leaders of a cause provide strategy and align people in common purposes.

Each of these components has strengths and weaknesses, so all are needed to fulfill God's plans for a strong, balanced, and effective church. Focusing on only one side of these truths will lead into falsehood. A nurturing community makes its members feel great, but families by nature are not geared to grow to unlimited size. Communities may become so inwardly focused that they never accomplish the purposes of God. The military structure of a cause works well at advancing the group's purposes, but without the care and support of family relationships, those soldiering on will eventually feel used and manipulated. A corporation can become impersonal when it focuses on tasks more than people, but without its organization, not much gets done. As in a motor vehicle, the engine must be connected to the transmission, or you will have a lot of noise but little forward movement!

When a problem arises in the church, the pastor needs to discern the nature of the problem—whether the issue is shepherding, managing, or leading. The pastor may have to dig for the true answer, but it will provide insight as to how to deal with the situation. Many problems that appear to focus on other issues will have real or perceived lack of shepherding at their roots.

Shepherding is Foundational

With everything I have said about the need for balance in the three aspects of pastoral ministry, I must assert that shepherding is foundational. The people and staff of Faith Community Baptist Church follow my leadership because they know I have a shepherd's heart for them. Even when I have to be firm and discipline people, they know I love them. A shepherd who loves and feeds the flock builds their trust.

I never lose sleep over money issues; it is God's responsibility to provide. I never worry about programs. But I agonize and lose sleep over lives. I cry over people with problems. I wake up in the middle of the night with a sense of desperation when I know people hurt. Their pain nearly kills me sometimes. More than once I have come to the Lord in torment over someone's situation, saying, "Lord, you can take away everything I have in ministry, but I want this person's life." Especially when someone is trapped in the deception of sin, I will pray hours for him or her. And what joy overwhelms me when I see a breakthrough!

Jesus' description of shepherding in John 10 shows that the greatest authority belongs to those who lay down their lives for their sheep. A pastor must understand this foundation and demonstrate it in daily life before pursuing apostolic leadership. Without a shepherd's heart, all else means nothing.

The Senior Pastor as Spiritual Leader

With this background on the nature of the pastoral ministry, let's take a closer look at the role of the senior pastor as spiritual leader, especially as this applies to the cell church. I asserted in chapter 2 that one of the prerequisites for successful transition to the cell church is a strong and God-anointed leader.

1. The Church is Led by One Anointed Person.

At the risk of their misunderstanding me as being arrogant, I have always told audiences around the world that one of the main factors contributing to the growth of Faith Community Baptist Church is the gracious gift of leadership the Lord has entrusted to me. FCBC has grown rapidly because of my strong and anointed leadership.

In the early years of the church, our leadership team carefully studied a chapter written by Oswald J. Smith in his book *Building a Better World*. He began his chapter with these words:

> "Behold, I have given him for a witness to the people, a leader and commander to the people" (Isa. 55:4). God's plan is that His flock should be led by a Shepherd, not run by a Board. Committees are to advise, never to dictate. The Holy Spirit appoints men. To Bishops and Elders is given the care of the churches, never to Committees. They are to be the Overseers, the Shepherds. Each one has his own flock. Because men have failed to recognize this, there has been trouble. When God's plan is followed, all is well.

Oswald Smith's chapter gave many illustrations from both Old and New Testaments. Yes, the church board has its place. Even the most anointed and God-appointed leaders will recognize their fallibility and need of others, so they will surround themselves with a team. Nevertheless, the board is not to rule, but to counsel. The board is not to dominate, but to support. The board is not to restrain, but to release the pastor into God's purposes. Otherwise, we violate God's pattern of leadership.

The cell group church is vision driven. It needs a strong leader to rally the people toward a God-given vision. Because it is also structured like the military, it calls for a strong commander to instill a sense of strict spiritual discipline needed to complete the task.

Traditionally, the church has been suspicious of strong leadership, especially when it is centered in one person. As a result, many human systems of checks and counterchecks have been built into traditional church polity to guard against one-person rule. Although I agree there is a need for mutual accountability, these checks have more often become major roadblocks for God's appointed leaders in their efforts to guide His people into victorious ministry.

Many lay leaders have expressed great fear of so-called "dictatorship" behind the pulpit. After more than 20 years of ministry, however, I must say that I have seen more "dictators" sitting in the pews than standing behind pulpits. Since the church is a voluntary society, people will not follow a dictatorial pastor. But the elderly lady who helped found the church, for instance, can often see to it that no one crosses her will.

Leadership is Not Dictatorship

Leadership means rallying people to pursue a vision. A leader successfully instills in those he or she is leading a deep desire to fulfill that vision. Leaders gain the trust of their people over time by virtue of their character, integrity, resourcefulness, zeal, good judgment, people skills, and—most important—their anointing from God. As a result, the people grant their leader the freedom to decide and the authority to supervise and control. Such leadership can never be provided by a committee or a board. If indeed such leadership is provided by a group, it is because within that group there is someone who can provide such strong leadership first to the group and through that to the rest of the people.

We often talk about New Testament leadership as if it were completely different from Old Testament leadership. I believe that biblical leadership is consistent throughout the Old and New Testaments, as well as Christian history. Whenever God wants to do a work, He chooses a person. The Old Testament showcases such leaders as Moses, Gideon, David, Elijah, and many others. In the New Testament, we have Peter as a leader for the Jews and Paul for the Gentiles. In Acts 11:22 we see the apostles in Jerusalem sending Barnabas to give leadership to the church in Antioch.

The priesthood of all believers does not negate this principle. Rather than a basis for church polity or leadership, the priesthood of all believers serves as a platform for moving in the power of the Holy Spirit. Effective leadership, however, rests in one God-anointed person. By and large, a church's maturity, spirituality, and influence will not rise above that of its leader.

Leadership in the Five-Fold Ministry

All five of the ministry roles specified in Ephesians 4:11–13 involve leaders, but each leads in a different way. The pastor leads as a caring shepherd with ability to build consensus. The teacher feeds the flock through teaching the Word. The evangelist strategizes for spiritual harvest and releases faith to the people to gather the ripe grain. The prophet imparts spiritual vision to the body and acts as a check to overall leadership. The apostle provides authoritative, visionary, and God-anointed leadership.

In recent years God has been restoring to the church the unique apostolic role. While an apostle does have pastoral skills to build consensus and forge a team around him or her, apostolic leadership operates by unction. The Lord Himself appoints and raises up generals in His army who will use that authority to equip and mobilize the body of Christ.

There is no doubt that Faith Community Baptist Church's tremendous growth comes as the result of God's special grace in and through my life. And because the church has recognized this God-given authority and freed me to exercise it, I have authority to empower others. As long as I walk humbly before the Lord in intimacy, the Lord will lead us from glory to glory.

I realize that as I promote and support strong apostolic leadership, the danger of abuse always exists. It is altogether possible for apostles to misuse the authority God has given us as His apostolic leaders. Nevertheless, this is apparently a risk God is willing to take with us because, in His grace, He has chosen to do just that. God is more than able to bring down His erring servants just as quickly as He raises them up.

Because God retains final control, we shouldn't spend too much time worrying about an apostle's ability to lead people astray, or building structures to rein in the extent of a leader's influence. No human system can ultimately constrain strong leaders anyway, because they learn how to beat the system. The real check on apostolic leaders lies in their relationship with the Lord. Those who have their hearts right with God will hear His voice when He speaks through others and will submit to His clear leading.

Instead of erecting systems that stifle strong leaders, we should commit to pray for them to stay in God's will. Then we can release them and trust them as people whom God has chosen. In 2 Corinthians 10:8 Paul, on behalf of himself and his fellow apostles, speaks of "the authority the Lord gave us for building you up rather than pulling you down." Apostolic leaders entrusted with this authority will feel a deep responsibility to look to God for direction in ministry, because the lives of many others rest in their hands.

2. The Church Must Allow the Pastor to Lead.

If a church will not allow its pastor to exercise authority in leadership, the pastor will often find ways to wrangle authority from the board or governing group through political moves. In such a situation, no one wins. A church that cannot trust its pastor with freedom to lead should release him or her to minister elsewhere.

Consider different kinds of church leadership. A church led solely by the congregation will stagnate at about 100 to 150 people. When all matters of the church must be decided at monthly congregational business meetings, church growth suffers because all ideas and decisions must wait for approval through this inefficient and time-consuming process. Not only that, congregational leadership means that a church's decision makers include brand-new Christians and carnal believers. This situation can hardly facilitate a church's growth, in either size or spirituality.

A church led by a lay board will accomplish more, but growth tends to taper off between 300 and 500 people. By that point, too many issues arise for the board to deal with at their meetings. The board begins to schedule more meetings that run longer and later, until the leaders stagger under the load. Moreover, when a lay board controls the pastoral staff, many full-time ministers eventually get frustrated and leave. When lay leaders have more authority, pastors may begin to feel their efforts are a waste of time. For the same reason, the church led by a lay board may have trouble attracting good people to the staff. This kind of church leadership can suggest a low view of the work of the kingdom—that any good lay leaders can do the job in their spare time. In fact, a dynamic and growing church requires a high level of professional staff to envision God's purposes for the church and implement local and global strategies to accomplish them.

Ideally, a church should be led by one God-anointed leader, together with a pastoral team that loves the Lord and desires His will. Such an arrangement will maximize the senior pastor's anointing to fulfill the vision God has given for the church. I believe the Lord will raise up such a leader when the people of the church humble themselves, when they commit to seeking God and His ways.

3. The Pastor Must Take Up the Role of Leadership.

Some pastors hesitate to lead their churches. They may feel they do not have a leadership gift. Or perhaps they do not want the responsibility of leadership. Some have played the religious game in churches long enough to conclude they would rather take a hands-off role when it comes to decision making. It's easier to let the lay board call the shots so people don't blame the pastor for problems and failures. Sometimes a senior pastor will drive the church staff crazy by not wanting to take leadership when it is badly needed.

A true leader will say, "The buck stops here." When a church gives its pastor freedom to lead and something doesn't work, the leader must be willing to stand humbly accountable before God and His people and admit mistakes. In fact, even if the failure is that of one of the staff members, the senior pastor is still responsible for approving the wrong choice of person in that role.

Every time a leader shares a vision with his or her people, that leader is making a promise and establishing a benchmark by which the people will measure him or her. The role of leadership carries awesome responsibility and should be taken on only with prayerful dependence on God. Humility and servant leadership characterize the best leaders and enhance their authority.

A strong leader determines God's purposes for the church and stands up with God-given conviction to guide the people into His will. Such leadership provides fertile ground for the church to grow and mature to unprecedented levels.

Leaders Need Affirmation with Humility

Many pastors have been hurt in leading. Their position makes them easy targets for arrows aimed at them from both within and outside of their congregation. Some have been blasted for past mistakes and then feel cut off, discouraged, unwilling to place themselves again in the line of fire.

I believe that God's leaders need affirmation and encouragement as they agree to take positions of leadership and responsibility. When people are willing to affirm, pray for, and release their leaders to become blessings to the body of Christ, God will give those leaders both the strength and the humility to serve.

When Faith Community Baptist Church started, my heart was completely shattered by the rejection of the leaders of my former church. The issues that finally brought about the split of the church turned personal. I was attacked for being controlling, dictatorial, and even dangerously influential. At the inception of FCBC, I had lost my confidence to lead. Thus I became laid back, relinquishing the leadership to my core leaders who, together with me, started the church.

In the beginning of 1987, a few months after the church started, we invited Pastor Bill Yaegar from the First Baptist Church of Modesto, California, to speak to us about leadership. Pastor Yaegar was in his 60s and since then has retired.

In his visit with us, Bill Yaegar noticed how discouraged I was. I could never forget his parting words to me at the Singapore airport. He said, "Son, I was praying for you this morning. The Lord told me He was giving you a new name. Your name shall be called 'Ari.' This is a Jewish name that means 'lion.'"

This word captivated me, because the name Singapore means "Lion City." The majestic cat is one of the cultural icons of our nation.

Pastor Yaegar went on, "Lawrence, the Lord tells you that you are the 'Lion of Singapore.' You are to stand up and roar. And whenever others forget that you are the 'Lion of Singapore,' stand up and roar again!"

No one had ever previously affirmed me that way. It was an extremely important moment in my ministry career. I realized in that instant that through all my years of Christian ministry, people were constantly warning me to go more slowly, to be more cautious, to be more "humble." This was the first time a seasoned servant of God had actually encouraged me to take charge, to lead, and to press on.

Something burst forth within the depths of my spirit. I have been roaring ever since for the glory of God and the advance of His kingdom!

ENCOURAGEMENT TO SENIOR PASTORS

In closing this chapter, let me share a few words of encouragement to senior pastors who doubt that they have the gift of leadership or enough God-given anointing to take the kind of role I am advocating. First of all, ask God for what you need. The Bible encourages us over and over to come to our Father and present our requests before Him. If He has called you to your position in your church, He is surely willing and able to give you all the resources you need to do the job.

If you ask the Lord for a leadership anointing and still feel that you just aren't wired that way, you may have a mismatch with your position. I would encourage you to ask God to raise up or send your church someone else with a gift of leadership. Then be courageous enough to relinquish your position and support this person, so the church's growth does not stagnate. If this radical change realigns both you and the church with God's highest purposes, everyone will come out a winner.

Senior pastors will also find that their anointing for leadership increases when they become part of an apostolic network. When you link with a group of churches under the apostolic covering and authority of a pioneer leader, your church will come alive.

The Roman centurion in Luke 7:1–10 understood this principle. He knew that the source of his effective and authoritative leadership over his soldiers and servants came from his own position under the authority of his commanding officers. The centurion also recognized that Jesus' authority derived from His submission to the supreme authority of His Father God.

Apostolic networks operate from this same premise. Today God has birthed more such networks than ever before in history, as the apostolic leadership role returns to prominence. I have begun forming an apostolic network of churches that will share a wider vision for world evangelization, as well as provide covering for churches that desire this link.

The church of Jesus Christ has a crying need for more strong, God-anointed leaders. As Bill Yaegar encouraged me, so let me encourage you, senior pastor. Remain in a close relationship of total submission to your sovereign Lord, so that you clearly hear His voice and direction. He will give you anointing and vision to lead those under your authority. Then, stand up and roar, for the glory of God and the advance of His kingdom!

Seven

REACHING OUT
AS A
COMMUNITY:

— *Evangelism in the Cell Church* —

I once read a story about a woman who received a medical examination from her family doctor. The doctor wrote her a prescription with the following instructions: "Take a red pill in the morning with a glass of water. Take a blue pill before lunch with a glass of water. Take a green pill before going to bed with a glass of water."

The worried woman's eyebrows furrowed. "Doctor, what's wrong with me?" she asked anxiously.

The doctor told her, "You just need to drink a lot more water."

Whatever can be said about evangelism, the bottom line is that we just need to do a lot more of it. Many churches have found that evangelism poses their greatest challenge. One of the most common questions asked by many pastors seeking to transition their congregations into cell churches is this: "How can we get every cell to multiply by evangelism?"

When a church first reorganizes itself into a cell structure, the initial multiplication of the cells comes largely from assimilation of existing members into the cell groups. For example, a 300-member church moving into the cell ministry might begin with perhaps three to five cells, involving about 40 to 70 members. These first five cells grow quickly because the cell members invite those worshiping in church on Sunday to join a cell. While some members will actively evangelize the lost, the majority of cell growth in the beginning will come the easy way—by incorporating existing members of the church.

The time will come when most members of the church have joined a cell. From then on, the only way for cells to grow and multiply is through active evangelism across the board. This poses a serious challenge, and most transitioning churches begin to stagnate in the growth of their cells at this point. The initial "grace" period may last anywhere from six months to two years, depending on the size of the church when it first begins the process of transitioning. So it is important to equip the whole church for active evangelism before this period runs out.

Let's examine the task of mobilizing the whole church in reaching the community for Christ. We will consider four simple questions:

1. What is a good map to use to understand evangelism?
2. What are the strategies we can adopt?
3. How do we equip members of the cells to evangelize?
4. How do we keep evangelism going?

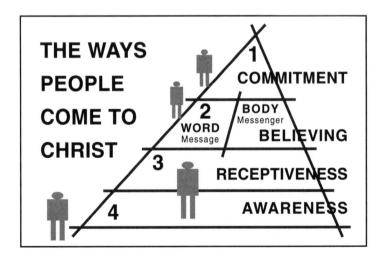

WHAT IS A GOOD MAP TO USE TO UNDERSTAND EVANGELISM?

The map used by Faith Community Baptist Church as a way of understanding the task of evangelism is the "Awareness Ladder," developed by Dr. Ralph Neighbour. This is a triangle demarcating the process of change in an unbeliever from an initial awareness of the gospel, to receptiveness, to believing, and finally to the point of commitment to Christ.

Many people in our societies remain unaware that the gospel has to do with a personal relationship with Jesus Christ. One of the key reasons for such ignorance is that they have never had meaningful contact with a true believer who has a vibrant faith in the Lord. Once an unbeliever becomes aware of the claims of the gospel, the next step is receptivity. Some people remain unreceptive because they don't see a need. Others stay closed because they have been exposed to some poor representation of Christ in the lives of believers. When an unbeliever becomes receptive to the gospel, however, the person may then enter a stage of seeking to believe. This phase involves studying both the content of the message as well as the consistency of the messenger. There is an examination of both the truths of the Bible and the authenticity of the body of Christ. As the non-Christian begins to believe in the message of the gospel as well as the messengers of the truth, this person comes to a point of committing his or her life to the Lord.

This model leads us to the helpful realization that people come to know the Lord in a process, and different unbelievers are at different stages of the process. Evangelism seeks to bring unbelievers from the level of awareness to the level of commitment. In so doing, we must learn to use different approaches with unbelievers at different levels.

One of the unfortunate mistakes of most evangelism methods is the assumption that every unbeliever is at the point of commitment. Evangelistic campaigns, for example, are really "harvest" events whose success depends upon how many unbelievers within the crowd are ripe and ready to make a commitment to Christ. Yet little is done to "cultivate" or work with unbelievers who will not be found in a religious meeting of this nature. Even more disturbing is the pyramid's illustration of how there are more people at the base than near the top. The church needs to develop different attitudes and different strategies for different levels of unbelievers.

In FCBC, we simplify this map by referring to two types of unbelievers. The type "A" unbeliever is someone either relationally or ideologically close to us. This means that the person is either open to the gospel or open to us. The type "A" unbeliever will be receptive to visiting a cell group because he or she is searching for the truth, or else perhaps is a close friend or relative of a cell member. By definition, a person who is willing to visit a cell or attend an evangelistic event is a type "A" unbeliever.

The type "B" unbeliever, on the other hand, is distant from us either relationally or ideologically. Such a person is open to neither the message of the gospel nor us as the messenger. This means we must go out of our way to look for this person in order to develop a relationship and bring him or her to a place of receptivity.

The heart of the Lord is clear. Ephesians 2:13 tells us that "in Christ Jesus you who once were far away have been brought near through the blood of Christ." We are commissioned to love those who are near (type "A" unbelievers) as well as those who are far (type "B" unbelievers). This map reveals to us not simply an evangelistic structure but the heart of God for all people.

WHAT ARE THE STRATEGIES WE CAN ADOPT?

The strategies of evangelism used at Faith Community Baptist Church could be summarized in the following statements:

1. We believe in community or body evangelism.
2. We are committed to relationship or "oikos" evangelism.
3. We are dedicated to servant evangelism.

Let's look at each of these in turn.

Body Evangelism

I introduced and discussed the concept of body evangelism in chapter 3. Traditional evangelism takes place one on one when a believer shares the gospel with an unbeliever, often in some form of booklet or memorized presentation. Body evangelism goes beyond this. It involves a group of believers or a cell reaching out to the lost together. The cell surrounds the unbeliever with the presence, the power, and the love of Christ. The cell demonstrates the reality of the gospel message in a tangible way to the unsaved. The group simply includes the unbeliever as part of the family, even before he or she makes a commitment to Christ.

Body evangelism involves a higher level of spiritual power, since the group prays in agreement for unbelievers and reaches out together rather than as individuals (see Matthew 18:19–20). In body evangelism, people with different gifts and personalities can all participate. In addition, going out as a body is often more fun and more natural than evangelizing one on one.

John, a staunch Buddhist in Singapore, was invited by a good friend to a cell meeting. The cell group had been praying for him for some time, and knew that John was resistant to the gospel. At the end of the cell meeting, the group encouraged John to give his life to the Lord. Although John was impressed by the fervent faith of the cell members, he rejected the invitation to receive Christ. He went on to say that unless God revealed Himself to him, he would not believe.

The group asked permission to pray for John, and he was willing. As the group gathered around him, they prayed earnestly that God would reveal Himself. The power of the Holy Spirit fell upon the man. John felt a power pinning him to the ground. Shocked, he asked the group what was happening. The members of the cell lovingly explained to him that God was answering their prayers in demonstrating His power in John's life. That evening, John gave his life to the Lord. Today, he is one of FCBC's cell leaders. The body of Christ surrounded John with the love and power of God in such a way that he could not help but admit, "Surely God is among you!" (see 1 Corinthians 14:25).

The Story of Gabriel

Consider another testimony of the power of body evangelism. The non-Christian brother of a cell member faced a crisis when his second son, Gabriel, was born. The doctors said that Gabriel had only 24 hours to live because half his heart was not functioning. Part of his head and his fingers had turned blue since delivery. The whole cell went to the hospital to pray for little Gabriel. The boy survived the first 24 hours, but the doctors nevertheless informed the parents that he had only a few days to live. No one had ever survived a similar condition for more than a few days, they said.

The cell members took turns visiting and praying for Gabriel and his parents. Gabriel not only survived but was discharged from the hospital, much to the astonishment of the doctors. Still, the doctors insisted that the baby would not live longer than three months. The cell group visited the home every Monday to pray for the boy. Gabriel's mother, Betty, received Christ as the result of the loving ministry of the whole cell.

Miraculously, Gabriel lived beyond three months. Eight months later, the heart valves opened that had been closed at birth. The heart chambers improved their functioning. The doctors began to believe that something could be done for Gabriel. Corrective heart surgery helped the baby's heart function more normally. A few days after the operation, Gabriel's father, who had been most skeptical of the gospel, felt so deeply touched by the love and power of God shining through the cell that he gave his life to the Lord.

Gabriel is now four years old. His parents attend one of our cell groups. Surrounded by the body of Christ, Gabriel and his parents experienced the reality of the gospel.

"Oikos" or Relationship Evangelism

The Greek word *oikos* literally means "household." Acts 16:31 says, "Believe in the Lord Jesus, and you will be saved—you and your household." When a person opens his heart to the Lord, he exposes his whole household to the gospel. We believe that "household" can refer to more than members of the immediate family. Rather, "oikos" identifies a network of the relationships in our lives. Our oikos includes not only our spouse and children but also our parents, siblings, uncles, aunts, neighbors, colleagues, tennis partners, and so on. Every member of the cell is taught to pray earnestly for every member of his or her oikos who does not know Jesus. We pray for open doors for the gospel of Jesus Christ into the lives of these oikos members.

Effective evangelism never happens in a vacuum. The greatest fruit comes when evangelism takes place through the network of relationships. How often do we knock on doors of strangers seeking to share the gospel, only to have doors closed in our face? I once heard a profound statement concerning evangelism that has stayed in my mind. It says, "People will not accept 'Someone' whom they do not know from someone whom they do not know." Working along oikos lines is the most natural way of sharing our faith in Jesus.

The Oikos of Janet and Jason

The following testimony illustrates the power of oikos evangelism. In 1993, a Christian couple returned from an overseas assignment to Hong Kong. Together with their cell leader, they visited a family facing a crisis. The lady of the house, Janet, together with her daughter, Mary, opened their hearts to the Lord. These two new converts joined another cell group near their home. Amazingly, a member of this cell group was a colleague of Janet's husband, Jason. In fact, the cell had been praying for Jason for a while and was delighted to receive his wife as a member of the cell.

Not long after that, Jason gave his heart to the Lord. His son, James, came to Christ the following weekend in the Sunday worship service. The next person who accepted the Lord in that family was James' mother-in-law. She was hospitalized, and the whole cell visited her to pray blessing and healing upon her. The manifested presence of the Lord around the hospital bed caused this elderly lady, a lifelong Taoist, to surrender her heart to Jesus. By the end of 1994, salvation had visited the whole household of Jason and Janet.

The story does not end there. As new members of the cell, Jason and Janet were taught to pray for those within their oikos who remained unbelievers. Together the Lord brought to their mind a good friend who used to baby-sit their children some years previously. They began praying for this friend's family. Jason and Janet invited them to a cell meeting designed especially for unbelievers. In that meeting, the son of this couple trusted the Lord. Later, the husband and wife also gave their lives to the Lord as the cell group helped them through some difficulties. After the husband, Brian, came to Christ, he became excited about his faith. At that time Brian was teaching a class of about 20 foreign workers from mainland China. He invited them to a barbecue and shared the Lord with them. Sixteen of these workers put their faith in the Lord that evening! By the middle of 1995, some 24 persons had trusted Christ since Janet's conversion— all because of oikos evangelism.

We have found that the average Christian has about eight to ten unbelievers within his or her oikos. Imagine a church of 100 believers reaching out to 1,000 unbelievers who are closely related to them. If just 10 percent of these unsaved come to know the Lord within the next 12 months, the church will double within the year.

Unfortunately, the more active in church believers become, the fewer unsaved friends they have within their oikos networks. This situation is especially pathetic among full-time ministers. Most find it difficult to identify even two or three unbelievers within their oikos. We have allowed the evil one to isolate us from unbelievers by means of religious activities. In Faith Community Baptist Church, we strongly recommend that our members not have any recreational activities unless there are unbelievers involved. We need to make acquaintance with non-Christians and then give those relationships time to build. As a pastor, I try constantly to develop friendships with unbelievers so they can be included within my oikos.

Servant Evangelism

Body evangelism has helped the members of FCBC to function as a community of cells. Oikos evangelism opens up many natural doors for the sharing of the gospel. As the cells move out in body evangelism, we find it is not enough to have open doors through oikos relationships. We must also have open hearts.

This brings us to servant evangelism. We in FCBC have been greatly blessed by Steve Sjogren's book *Conspiracy of Kindness*. He crystallized for us in words something we had been doing—teaching our believers to demonstrate God's love to the unsaved in practical ways through acts of kindness with no strings attached.

Steve in his book discusses the arena of the heart and how servant evangelism touches the hearts of unbelievers:

> The *Evangelical Dictionary of Theology* defines "heart" in the biblical sense as meaning "the center or focus of man's personal life, the spring of all his desires, motives, and moral choices—indeed, of all his behavioral trends." Thus, when we touch the heart, we have touched a person at the deepest level.

The exciting news is that the heart isn't unreachable. Our experience has shown that a person's heart is most quickly touched by acts of service....

Servant evangelism enables us to quickly touch the heart—the decision-making center of a person's life—and make a lasting impact. If the human heart is the ultimate target of our evangelism, why not shoot for the heart from the first moment of our encounter with non-Christians? (pp. 112–113)

Acts of Service Open Doors and Hearts

In one of our university campus hostels, a cell group decided to wash the toilets of the dormitory as an act of kindness. The unbelievers living in that hostel were surprised. They became aware of the presence of the cell group meeting regularly for worship in their dormitory. A week later, a knock came on the door of the room while a cell meeting was in progress and a young lady asked, "Can you tell me how I could be a Christian?" With great joy, the cell led her to the Lord.

In January 1997 FCBC organized a neighborhood clean-up for Chinese New Year. Cell members knocked on doors within the high-rise housing developments and asked if they could help clean the flats. In the process they made many new friends, including an elderly woman who told them a remarkable story. "I had a dream four years ago," she said. "I was lined up in heaven but was told I was in the wrong line because I didn't have the key. Ever since then I've been asking people, 'What is this key?'" The cell members took the opportunity to tell her about Jesus as the key to heaven. The woman gave her heart to Christ that very day.

Servant evangelism has a powerful impact because it touches people's hearts and moves them higher on the Awareness Ladder map. Those who are not ready to commit or even to believe will become more receptive to the gospel because God's people have showed them His love through acts of kindness with no strings attached.

HOW DO WE EQUIP MEMBERS OF THE CELLS TO EVANGELIZE?

The map we use has set the challenge of evangelism before us. The strategies determine the approaches by which the whole cell can be involved. Now, every member needs to be trained to embark upon the task of winning others for Christ. We must put in their hands some equipment or tools for the job. In Faith Community Baptist Church, these tools include:

1. Being part of a cell.
2. Type "A" evangelism training.
3. Spiritual warfare training.
4. Type "B" evangelism training.

Let's take a closer look at each of these tools.

1. Being Part of a Cell

We have found that just putting someone into a spiritual healthy cell begins the process of training that person for evangelism. In the cell, we have developed an atmosphere for evangelism in which all members are ministers. During the Works portion of every cell meeting, the cell prays for unbelievers. In addition, we hold periodic harvest events in which the unsaved are invited to a cell meeting where members share the gospel in a relational way. The cell literally breathes, talks, dreams, and does evangelism, modeling it for newcomers. Anyone in a cell long enough will be "infected" by a highly contagious, incurable, and almost terminal case of "evangelitis"! The cell causes its members to cultivate a lifestyle of evangelism and gain confidence that God can use them in this way.

This lifestyle is more important than any other training we can give a believer.

2. Type "A" Evangelism Training

FCBC has set up a spiritual boot camp called "The Year of Equipping" for all believers who come to the church. I will discuss this more completely in chapter 9. Within this spiritual boot camp is type "A" evangelism training. New believers attend a seminar that runs all day Saturday in which they are given four important tools:

a) *The Awareness Ladder and the concept of type "A" and type "B" unbelievers.*

b) *The "oikos" principle.*

All new believers prepare a list of unbelievers within their oikos network of relationships. They commit themselves to begin praying for the salvation of these unbelievers.

c) *The one-minute personal testimony.*

Every cell member is trained to prepare a personal testimony of his or her conversion that can be shared in one minute. The testimony begins with these words: "Let me tell you the greatest thing that has ever happened to my life...." It ends with the question, "Has that ever happened to you?" This testimony is kept to one minute so that by the time an unbeliever switches off, the believer has finished sharing. The last question seeks to open a door of discussion about spiritual issues.

d) *The John 3:16 presentation.*

This tool gives a relational way of sharing the gospel using a simple "bridge" diagram that a person can draw on a piece of paper. This concept originated with Dr. Ralph Neighbour. In FCBC, we have adopted this model as our way of presenting the gospel to an unbeliever who is at the point of commitment. We use it for people who respond to the gospel invitation at our public meetings as well as for leading someone to the Lord in our cell gatherings.

3. Spiritual Warfare Training

We believe strongly that in order to preach the gospel effectively, we must look to God for signs and wonders done in the power of the Holy Spirit. Every member of Faith Community Baptist Church is trained to move in the gifts of the Holy Spirit and to minister to others in the power of the Lord. This training gets carried out over two weekends.

In the first weekend, we pray over everyone in attendance to receive the infilling of the Holy Spirit. Those who have yet to speak in tongues gain an impartation of the prayer language of the Spirit. The various gifts of the Holy Spirit are taught, demonstrated, and released upon the people. We take considerable time to teach every person how to move in prophecy and words of knowledge. Everyone is trained to operate in faith by learning to listen to the Holy Spirit's prompting. During this weekend many opportunities emerge to pray for people's needs that surface as the result of divine revelation.

In the second weekend, we focus on praying for the sick. FCBC uses the five-step model developed by Pastor John Wimber. Some people become sick because of sin in their lives. In that weekend, the Holy Spirit will reveal such root causes. The people learn to lead others into confession of their sins and to release forgiveness to them on the basis of the cross of Christ. When this takes place, many sicknesses are healed instantly. In addition, people find freedom from many spiritual strongholds in their lives. We also deal with sicknesses that result from emotional wounding in the past. As the Holy Spirit brings healing to these past hurts, more people are set free from chronic illnesses.

The most dramatic part of this second weekend comes in teaching every person how to cast out demons. We demonstrate how this is done with the permission of a new believer known to have demonic strongholds. As we confront the power of darkness, generations of demons will manifest, not only in the person receiving prayer but also in many other believers attending the seminar. In Singapore, most of us are first-generation believers. We carry in our family line the curses of idolatry committed by previous generations. In fact, many people were dedicated to demons at birth. As these spiritual ties get severed, demons begin to manifest. We call on the name of the Lord, clearly demonstrating the power and authority of the cross. Every person leaves the seminar with hands-on experience in ministering deliverance to the demonized. Even more important, they leave having experienced the power of the cross over demonic forces.

After this spiritual warfare training, we encourage every person to move in the gifts of the Spirit in the cell groups. They are admonished to minister to one another in the power of the Lord when needs surface within the cells. Beyond that, we release them into the community as ministers of the gospel. We commission them to heal the sick, cast out demons, and preach the gospel of the kingdom.

4. Type "B" Evangelism Training

When members of the cell develop a lifestyle of evangelism, actively sharing the gospel with people in their oikos network, they are ready to minister to type "B" unbelievers—people whom the cell members have to go out of their way to reach.

The challenge in working with type "B" unbelievers is that no one method will ensure success. Years ago in FCBC, we tried all sorts of evangelistic programs. We trained our people to host ten-week "Friendship Groups," "Share Groups," and "Interest Groups" focused on some common interest, subject, or need. We have found these programs rigid and even awkward at times. Success rate was minimal. What's worse, most of my people considered the methods stifling and I could not motivate them to continue.

A new perspective arose as the Lord began to teach us about strategic intercession for the nation through Dr. C. Peter Wagner of Global Harvest Ministries. He also sent other servants of God to teach us about prayerwalks. Prayerwalking means physically walking the land and praying for the people—"praying on site with insight," according to the book *Prayerwalking* by Steve Hawthorne and Graham Kendrick. Walking is by itself a way for us to get out of our homes and into the community we are called to pastor. Then as we walk, God will show us needs and prompt us to pray for them. We will also see ways we can serve people through acts of kindness.

The Lord then began to use me to provide leadership for the Spiritual Warfare Network in Singapore. This movement unites the churches of Singapore to pray for revival, identify the strongholds of the land, repent over the sins associated with these strongholds, and tear down these demonic constructs through fervent, united prayers. The final chapter of this book discusses some warfare strategies to repossess the city.

Through these new paradigms, the Lord taught us in FCBC to mobilize the cells to reach out to type "B" unbelievers beyond our oikos networks. First we must find some way to make contact with these unbelievers and bring them into our oikos, or at least soften resistance within an environment so people become open to our efforts to share the gospel. What we have learned to do for the whole nation in strategic intercession we began to apply on the level of the individual cell groups, in order to help them win their neighborhoods, their offices, and their schools for the Lord. Each cell group is taught to prayerwalk their neighborhood, discover strongholds in the area, and hear from the Lord as to how to bless or serve the people there. These efforts open previously closed doors for preaching the gospel, and have given our people powerful tools to penetrate any environment with the Good News of Jesus Christ.

In the type "B" evangelism training weekend, every person receives teaching on the principles and practice of prayerwalking, the skill of discerning spiritual strongholds in a given area, how to develop sensitivity to the leadership of the Holy Spirit, and how to find occasions to bless and serve people. As a result, countless opportunities emerge for the cells to win the unsaved for Jesus Christ.

How Do We Keep Evangelism Going?

Maintaining a lifestyle of evangelism can seem like a heavy burden. For most traditional, program-based congregations, outreach takes place once a year during the annual evangelistic campaign. About a month prior to the campaign, the pastor and the evangelism committee push with all their wits to get members to invite their friends to this special event. They assure people that the invited speaker is an anointed evangelist and that this year's program will surpass all the rest. The members of the church need confidence that any unsaved friends they bring will not be disappointed or embarrassed by the quality of the meeting. Everybody works hard to make this evangelistic event a success. Prayer plays a major role.

The day arrives. The auditorium is packed. Unbelievers constitute about one-third of those in attendance—a major success. The rest are Christians from either the host church or other churches who want to check out the speaker or watch this great program they have heard advertised. The evangelist preaches his heart out. More than five percent of the unbelievers respond to the altar call. Everyone marvels at the outstanding response—better than anything they have seen in the past. No doubt this has been a good year for the church.

Afterwards, the host church makes efforts to follow up the new converts. If they really work hard at it, the church retains about three to five percent of all those who responded to the invitation during the evangelistic meetings. This is more or less the "industrial average" for most churches. After such a great time, everyone in the church rejoices over the great blessings received from the Lord. The normal programs of the church resume. Evangelism as a church-wide effort gets shelved until the same time next year.

I have no doubt that anyone who has ministered in a traditional church can identify with the above scenario. I know, because I have been a successful pastor of a fast-growing traditional church. But does this scenario represent the best we have to hope for? How can the pace of evangelism be kept up all year round? How can we be like the New Testament church, in which "the Lord added to their number daily those who were being saved" (Acts 2:47)?

The answer is found in the cell church. In Faith Community Baptist Church, we have developed an environment and culture for evangelism to flourish as a lifestyle. We have built ongoing ministries that reach out to every receptivity level of unbelievers all the time. The cell church is like a big net that we have placed carefully in the community in order to fish and catch men and women for the kingdom of God. To use another analogy, the cell church structure has become a giant engine perpetually driving the church into strategic, active, and continuous evangelism.

Evangelism need not seem like a heavy stone that is hard to move. With the proper nudge of leadership and planning, the cell church structure will create the momentum that begins propelling evangelism efforts into the whole community.

The diagram on the next page shows the different levels of evangelistic activities of FCBC seeking to bring an unbeliever from the community into the church. The closer these activities are to the community at large, the less religious they become. At the initial "touch points" with the community, the outreach efforts may be completely non-religious in nature and almost exclusively geared to meet people's felt needs. As unbelievers are drawn toward the Lord, the nature of the evangelistic activities becomes more spiritual and seeks to highlight the real need of every person for salvation in Jesus Christ. Let's consider each of these levels in greater detail.

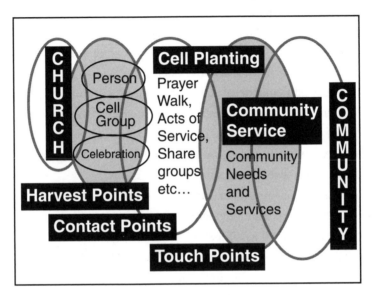

1. Harvest Points—Cycles of Harvest

The evangelistic level closest to the church consists of harvest points. At these points unbelievers will make a commitment to Jesus Christ. The church is constantly winning the unsaved for the Lord through the personal witness of every believer, the combined efforts of the cell groups, as well as large-scale "celebration" events on weekends or special occasions.

One of the most powerful engines for growth in FCBC is what we call the "cycles of harvest." Each year, FCBC builds into the calendar three cycles of harvest. The first cycle begins in January and ends at the Easter weekend in early spring. The second cycle commences in June and finishes with a large evangelistic campaign in a sports stadium toward the end of August. The third and final cycle of the year begins in October and runs until Christmas. These cycles of harvest serve as both a powerful tool for ingathering the lost as well as an effective equipping and motivating strategy for the cells. They constitute the heartbeat of the church, enabling us to maintain a vibrant momentum for evangelism.

A typical cycle of harvest has three components: (a) a culminating harvest event, (b) an initial weekend of type "A" evangelism training, and (c) about ten weeks of practice, prayer, and preparation in the cell.

a) Harvest Event:

In the early 1990s, God showed us that we should do a cell-based harvest event. Prior to this, we organized a few series of large evangelistic meetings throughout the year. We booked the 12,000-seat Singapore Indoor Stadium and packed it with unbelievers four or five times in a week. Many responded to the altar call each night. When the Lord spoke to us about having cell-based harvest, however, every cell faced a monumental challenge. The plan involved having each cell organize a special Good Friday service in the home. The cells invited the unsaved for this special gathering. We carefully planned this meeting for every cell so that it would present the gospel in a personal and sensitive manner. At the end of the program, every cell member shared the gospel one on one to the friends he or she brought to the cell.

This kind of harvest event has turned out to be no less effective than a campaign in a huge stadium. In 1998, at the Good Friday event called "Thank God It's Friday" (T.G.I.F.), a total of 483 cell meetings took place. In that one evening, a total of 9,884 people attended the cells. That figure included 3,833 visitors, of which 2,897 were unbelievers. Compare this to mass evangelistic crusades when we have had 10,000 people in one place and cannot be sure there are that many unsaved among the crowd. Here in one evening, 2,897 unbelievers came, each personally invited by a cell member. Each of these unbelievers experienced the presence of God in the cell and received a personal presentation of the gospel. No wonder, in that one evening, we logged 517 conversions, accounting for almost 18 percent of the unbelievers present.

Our summer cycle of harvest is a church-based campaign with large stadium meetings. We also hold another cell-based harvest event in December called "I'll Be Home for Christmas." In 1998, a total of 625 people accepted the Lord in that one cell-based event. Even more startling, 13,167 people attended cell groups that week, well outstripping the capacity of Singapore Indoor Stadium!

b) Weekend Training:

The harvest event represents the climax of the harvest cycle, when every believer has the opportunity of sharing the gospel with an unbeliever whom he or she has invited to the cell or to a meeting in a stadium. The success of these harvest events depends on the people being properly equipped for the process.

The cycle of harvest begins with a weekend of type "A" evangelism training, described earlier in the chapter. Cell leaders encourage every cell member who has not gone through this training to sign up for this event. As mentioned before, all those who attend the type "A" evangelism training will be equipped with the basic tools to share the gospel with people in their oikos networks of relationships.

c) Ten Weeks of Preparation:

This is the most important part of the harvest cycle. It connects the initial weekend evangelism training to the harvest event at the end of the cycle. In the intervening ten weeks, the Works segments of the cell meetings are specially designed to fulfill two purposes.

First, the skills taught in the weekend training get practiced. The week following the evangelism seminar, the cell leader asks those who attended to describe how the training has been helpful. In subsequent weeks, the group reviews the oikos list of every cell member. The cell provides opportunities to practice the one-minute testimony and the John 3:16 presentation within the cell meeting. Members also receive assignments to share the testimony or the gospel with an unsaved friend in their oikos. While it's best to share in a natural way, they may break the ice by telling the nonbeliever, "I have a class assignment I need to complete. Can you help me? I need to give you this presentation and ask for your response." In the process, many people will get saved even before the harvest event.

During these weeks of preparation, those who recently completed the weekend training develop the skill of sharing the gospel. We believe that training takes place not just in a seminar but through practice under supervision. The final test will come with the sharing of the John 3:16 presentation during the impending harvest event. At the same time, those who previously went through the weekend training are again challenged and mobilized to keep evangelism active in their lives. In addition, those who have yet to attend the training learn within the cell both the need to share the gospel and the skill required to do so. This season becomes a powerful equipping time in the cell when the fire of evangelism gets continuously fueled.

Second, during the Works segment of the cell meeting, cell members also begin to pray for unbelievers within their oikos whom they plan to invite to the coming harvest event. Cell leaders follow up on people's progress in issuing these invitations. Increasing time is spent praying for the harvest event and the invited guests as the special day approaches. By the time of the harvest event, all members have honed their skills in sharing the gospel, and the event as well as the guests have been thoroughly covered with prayer. This process conveys a special anointing for evangelism on every harvest event of FCBC.

As these cycles of evangelism recur three times every year, the members of FCBC receive continual equipping as well as enthusiasm for the work of evangelism among type "A" unbelievers.

2. Contact Points—Cell Planting

As the whole body becomes mobilized to reach out to the type "A" non-believers within the oikos of each member, the church enjoys a quantum leap in growth. Nevertheless, we should cast the net even more widely. We must make constant efforts to penetrate into new oikos networks or "marketplaces" with the gospel. This is type "B" evangelism. It requires a commitment to get out of our comfort zones and be willing to move into another oikos in order to share the gospel of Christ.

I mentioned earlier that when a church begins to transition into the cell church structure, the initial growth of the cells comes by assimilation of existing members into the groups. When almost every person in the church has joined a cell, the church will face stagnation in growth unless every cell is equipped and mobilized for evangelism.

In our experience at Faith Community Baptist Church, we put in place the equipping system and the cycles of harvest in order to propel the church forward in evangelistic outreach toward the people in the oikos of each cell member. After a few years of rapid growth, however, the multiplication of the cells gradually slowed toward a halt.

As I sought the Lord about what was going on, I happened to "stumble" upon an interesting web site about biological cells. What I read there gave me a revelation from the Lord!

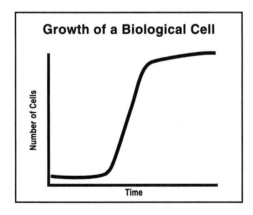

The article in the web site explained why biological cells cannot keep on multiplying indefinitely. Apparently, when a cell is cultured in a specific environment, the first few generations of cell multiplication take somewhat longer than normal, as they overcome some inertial factors. Then the cells begin to proliferate, multiplying like clockwork in regular intervals. However, after a period of time dependent on the size of the environment, the rate of multiplication begins to decrease. In other words, it takes a progressively longer period for a new generation of cells to develop. The crucial reason: Biological cells stagnate in growth because they exhaust the nutrients in their environment. In fact, a time comes when, for each cell that multiplies, another cell dies. Growth stops and cells remain in a state of equilibrium—perhaps even begin to decline in number—unless their environment receives a new injection of nutrients.

Breaking Out of Stagnation

I immediately recognized this pattern in FCBC. Our initial multiplication of cells had been somewhat challenging. We needed to cast the vision for the people, equip them for the task, and allow time to work through the initial "bugs." Then for the next four years, cells multiplied regularly by evangelism, sparking a growth explosion in the church. After that, the average time needed to multiply a cell began to increase until stagnation in cell growth ensued. The reason was easily traced: The cells had exhausted the oikos relationships of group members, given the specific location of the cell and the nature of the group. In other words, all unbelievers within the oikos networks of members had either come to the Lord or rejected any further attempts to share Christ with them.

The Lord began to show me that the way to break out of this stagnation was to mobilize all the cells in aggressive cell planting. Cell planting involves intentionally seeking to start a new cell in a new environment. This environment could be a new cell location, or a new target consisting of a specific kind of people sharing common needs or common functions. Those sharing common needs could include single parents, cancer patients, or teenage delinquents. Groups of people sharing common functions might consist of blue-collar workers, taxi-drivers, lawyers, and so on. I will discuss cell planting in more detail in the next chapter.

Every cell is challenged to plant a cell in addition to reaching out to their own oikos people. Cell-planting teams of two or three persons from each cell seek the Lord as to both location and target group of outreach. In 1998, we designated the second cycle of harvest as a cell-planting cycle. The cell leaders came together regularly to pray, to share what the Lord was doing, and to exchange ideas they learned in cell-planting attempts. Within four months, some 115 new cells were planted, with another 114 active cell-planting efforts in progress.

3. Touch Points—Community Service

The furthest reach of the evangelistic arm of our church extends to what we call touch points, when we go out on a limb to touch the needy in our community. Let's recapitulate: We have cells running harvest cycles and actively sharing the gospel to type "A" unbelievers. In addition, we have cell-planting efforts seeking to penetrate into new locations or among new groups of people. The final connection involves community service programs that minister to the needy on every level of society. Because these touch points represent our initial contact with the community, they are neutral and non-religious in nature.

FCBC has set up TOUCH Community Services (TCS), a voluntary welfare organization staffed by professionals but supported by Christian volunteers from the church. The distinctiveness of TCS is that its programs are completely non-religious. For example, we run two childcare centers in Singapore, and we do not allow these centers to sing any Christian songs. The reason is that the minute we sing religious songs, the Buddhists, Hindus, and Muslims will not send their children to these childcare centers, defeating our purpose to touch the lives of Singaporeans who have no receptivity to the church. Naturally, while the programs themselves are neutral, the volunteers are Christians. And when these believers perform acts of service for the needy and underprivileged in society, they find countless open doors to share the gospel of Christ.

We began in 1988 with a simple after-school club for latchkey children in a primary school. Today, we have more than 16 professionally-run service centers spread throughout Singapore. Our services include childcare centers, learning centers for intellectually disabled children, the latchkey children's center, children's clubs, youth services for delinquents, welfare services, legal aid services, community counseling, marriage counseling, home care for the aged, an activity center for the aged, handicapped centers, a handicapped hostel, a "silent club" (for the deaf), a diabetes support association, and healthcare services for the poor. We also produce one of Singapore's most well-known magazines on family issues.

Our community services have found so much favor with government authorities that much of our service ministry is actually funded by the government. As of now, the juvenile courts make it mandatory for certain offenders to seek help from our youth counseling services. Also, the registry of marriage has invited us to conduct premarital counseling for all who are getting married in Singapore. This is our "root system" into the unconverted world.

Our goal is that TOUCH Community Services becomes a household name in our country by the year A.D. 2000. Its programs, together with the other levels of evangelism, will form a net to draw the people of Singapore into the kingdom of God.

EVANGELISM IS THE WORK OF A COMMUNITY

In summary, one statement highlighting the whole concept of evangelism in a cell church seems to say it all: Evangelism is the work of a community.

In Matthew 4:19 we read, "'Come, follow me,' Jesus said, 'and I will make you fishers of men.'" I remember my Sunday school teacher teaching me that little chorus, with its casting motions: "I will make you fishers of men, if you follow me." Many times I heard reminders that as believers we must all be fishers of men and women, boys and girls. Frankly, this admonition often left me with a sense of guilt. My idea of being a fisherman was to go "rod fishing" for unbelievers, one at a time. This traditional concept of evangelism tends to have a "gotcha" mentality. The guilt level becomes unbearable when other Christians give testimony about the number of "fish" they have caught.

I believe we have not often examined the context of Jesus' words. In the preceding verse, we read, "...They were casting a net into the lake, for they were fishermen." When Jesus called us to be fishers, He called us to a fishing community. When a fishing community goes out to sea, each person has a different role. Whatever the role may be, each person enjoys equal share in the fish caught.

Matthew 13:47–48a says, "...the kingdom of heaven is like a net that was let down into the lake and caught all kinds of fish. When it was full, the fishermen pulled it up on the shore...." When evangelism is understood in this light, we see that each of us contributes a vital component of the spiritual fishnet for winning the lost. This corporate responsibility releases us from unnecessary guilt and frees us to be all that God has made us to be in the wonderful task of sharing the gospel. Let's get on with this task as a community of believers, casting the spiritual net of God's love, power, and truth to haul in a mighty catch for the kingdom of God!

Eight

REAPING BEYOND THE BORDERS:

— *Cell Planting for Greater Harvest* —

In the previous chapter I told the story of how I was surfing the Internet one day and happened upon a web site that described the reproductive cycles of biological cells. I immediately saw how the process portrayed there mirrored the cell growth cycles we had experienced in Faith Community Baptist Church. No doubt the Lord Himself brought this cyberspace information to my attention, because it came at a time when the church was desperate not only to maintain cell growth, which had been slowing over the previous couple of years, but also to seek explosive growth. The insight He gave me through this web site brought FCBC an important piece in the puzzle of church growth strategies: cell planting.

Cell planting requires its own worldview shift—a paradigm within the paradigm of the cell church model. We learned that we need to go beyond the old strategies and their built-in limitations if we want to reach previously unpenetrated segments of society. This, after all, is the heart of God—relentlessly pursuing His beloved lost sheep who remain outside the confines of the sheep fold.

In this chapter we will explore four key aspects of the cell-planting strategy: the concept, core methods, common targets, and critical steps in the cell-planting process.

CONCEPT: WHAT IS CELL PLANTING?

Cell planting stands in contrast to simple cell multiplication, which is the process of enlarging existing communities. In cell multiplication, an existing cell grows by incorporating people until it becomes big enough to multiply into two cells. Cell planting, on the other hand, involves establishing new communities that do not spring out of a group's natural growth. To plant a cell, believers must go out and reach new people in new environments to form a new group. Both kinds of growth are needed.

Cell planting works hand in hand with type "B" evangelism. In cell planting we invade new territory for the kingdom of God. In most cases, this kind of outreach poses a greater challenge for leaders than multiplying current cells. The rewards, however, are proportionately greater, because we can reach people for Jesus Christ who would have little likelihood of joining existing cell communities.

Powerful testimonies abound. A cell church in Bogotá, Colombia, pastored by César Castellanos, used the cell-planting strategy to grow the church from a single cell group to 90,000 people in ten years. Phenomenal growth continues to this day. Every member receives training to reach out to new people and plant new cells.

Why is cell planting needed? As FCBC has launched into this approach, we see four reasons.

1. Cells Do Not Multiply Indefinitely.

The web site discussion about the reproduction of biological cells yielded the important discovery that cells do not multiply indefinitely. If they did, our adult bodies by now would weigh several thousand kilograms, and counting! As I described in the previous chapter, a biological cell's first generations of growth come slowly as significant energy is required to overcome inertia. Then after passing this initial stage, cells proliferate in rapid and regular multiplication. As time goes on, growth tapers off and the cells stagnate because they have exhausted the nutrients around them. For each cell that grows, another dies. Eventually, the nutrients cannot even sustain equilibrium, and more aging cells begin to die as toxins creep into the system.

This is the natural cycle of life with biological cells. When I recognized signs of this process in Faith Community Baptist Church, I realized that our slowing growth did not necessarily indicate a fatal flaw in our methods. While we certainly made some mistakes in training and equipping people, more fundamentally the church was simply going through a natural stage of the life cycle. Growth of the cell groups had begun to stagnate because cell members had exhausted most of their near-contact oikos relationships. These unbelievers had either come to Christ and joined a cell already, or put up barriers of resistance. Rather than fighting against a natural process, we needed to look beyond our current paradigm to see how to inject more "nutrients" into the system. While we prayed for a mighty revival of the Holy Spirit, God encouraged us to initiate a more intentional strategy of cell planting through type "B" evangelism.

2. Some Converts Cannot Be Assimilated into Existing Cells.

Faith Community Baptist Church has achieved an assimilation rate of approximately 20 percent of the converts won by our church. My understanding is that the average retention and assimilation rate, worldwide, stands at about five percent of new Christian converts. We praise God for the success He has given us, but we are not satisfied. We want more. We have discovered, however, that the usual cell multiplication model has built-in limitations.

While many people who come to know the Lord in the context of a cell group will join the cell because of current relationships with members, some new converts have barriers to assimilation in existing groups. Perhaps a businessman won a colleague for Christ, but cannot easily invite this man to join his own cell group because he lives all the way across town. The new convert hesitates to join a group in his own area because he knows no believers there.

One of our cell members who serves as a school teacher began to lead students to Christ. At one "Thank God It's Friday" harvest event, 25 children came to know the Lord. While we have intergenerational cell groups in which children and adults fellowship together, participation assumes that parents allow their children to come. And in many cases, non-Christian fathers or mothers choose not to give this permission. How do we assimilate 25 young new believers whose parents have not yet trusted Christ?

Assimilation proves difficult when new converts come from a different stratum of society, age group, locality, culture, or language background from the majority of the cell. A professional woman who, by God's grace, leads a couple of factory workers to the Lord will have trouble folding them into her own cell group if the rest of the cell reflects an upper income bracket. The same is true for converts who do not speak the same language as the cell group of the person who evangelized them. FCBC tried having bilingual cells, but they didn't work for us because the translation process hindered group dynamics. Cells need more of a family atmosphere in which relationships can be personal and spontaneous.

In most situations like these, incorporating new believers will require planting new cells for them. It is far easier for new believers from similar backgrounds to join together in a freshly formed group than to try to fit into an existing group filled with people with whom they may not feel comfortable.

3. Cell Planting is Needed for Explosive Growth.

God has given Faith Community Baptist Church a vision to establish 5,000 cells by the year 2000. This goal is humanly impossible. We worked hard for more than 13 years (eleven of them as a cell church) and grew to more than 800 cells, but the same rate and same methods will not bring us anywhere near the 5,000 mark so soon. Yet we believe God wants us to do it, so we must find His ways.

The Lord has given us a strategy. The math shows us that we can hit the target if every cell doubles by the end of 1999 and then each of these begins four cell-planting efforts, quadrupling by the end of 2000. How can this possibly be accomplished? Both cell multiplication and cell planting are needed, but we believe cell planting in particular provides a platform to reach the unreached community with explosive growth. Since we officially launched the cell-planting program in July 1998, we are already on our way to achieving the goal of doubling. The Holy Spirit must continue to empower this effort through widespread revival.

4. Cell Planting Helps Us Target the Whole City.

Through ordinary cell multiplication, cell members saturate their oikos networks so that everyone among their near-contact relationships has the opportunity to hear and respond to the gospel of Christ. But what about those outside the oikos? Unless two circles intersect, the gospel cannot flow freely from one to another. Moreover, some groups of people may remain outside the awareness of believers, who do not even realize whole segments of society have no Christian witness in their midst.

Cell planting enables the church to target the whole city cell by cell. Research will help us discover what demographic groups and locales still need their own cells. Then believers can begin to move out of their communities into new communities with a systematic plan of planting cells to reach every neighborhood, every housing complex, every school, every military camp, every work group, every age group.

CORE METHODS: HOW DO WE PLANT A CELL?

In FCBC's short experience with cell planting, we have explored three core methods of planting new cells that have proved workable. By God's grace we hope to discover more ways.

1. The Cell Supports a Cell-Planting Team.

Suppose not everyone in a cell group is ready to plant a new cell. Although my desire is for every cell member to have a missionary heart to extend the kingdom of God, I recognize that we aren't there yet. So meanwhile, the cell might choose to set apart a few people and through them send out a "runner" into the community. These two or three people, trained in type "B" evangelism, survey their target community and begin to make contact with non-believers there. While they pray and build relationships with the unsaved, they remain part of their sending cell in order to receive intercession and empowering. The cell-planting team reports on their progress during the Works stage of their cell meeting and receives support from the sending cell. Then as the team begins to see people give their lives to Christ, they gather a group of these converts to form the core of a new cell.

One cell group sent out three people to lead a ten-week conversational English class for speakers of Cantonese or other dialects. They started with the parents of latchkey children who attended the same school as their own kids. When they finished the class, the relationships they had built enabled the team to continue nurturing friendships with these people. They went to karaoke clubs together to enjoy an evening of singing. They took weekend tours to Malaysia. Then when the team felt they had forged strong links with the group, they suggested getting together for prayer, sharing, and worship. Starting with three Christians and ten non-Christians, they planted a cell that included the complete cell agenda, with all Four W's.

Soon this team had opportunity to pray for felt needs and see God's answers. One woman shared that her son had come down with chicken pox. The group prayed in Jesus' name, and by the next day he was totally healed of symptoms. The mother declared with awe, "Your God is really powerful!" One by one the entire group gave their lives to Christ through similar experiences. In the four years since the original cell sent out this team, they have commissioned a total of four teams and seen four new cells planted.

2. The Whole Cell Plants a New Cell.

In the second method of cell planting, the whole cell group sees a need for a Christian witness among a segment of unbelievers. The entire cell commits to being a missionary team. They may start by sending out a team of two or three to survey an area or a community subgroup to discover their needs, make contact with people, and perhaps win an initial convert or two. While the team may not yet have received enough response to form the core group of a new cell, they do not want new believers or prospects to drift away without receiving nurture. So at this point, the whole cell comes and plants themselves among this community to "jump-start" a new cell. In this way they provide a place for new converts or seekers to experience the power of the Lord in Christian fellowship. Furthermore, the cell group dynamics ensure that the new believers receive vision and motivation to reach their own community for Christ.

One cell group that met in a neighborhood of low-rise terraced houses felt burdened for a condominium complex a few minutes away with no cell in its midst. The group discovered that a member of Faith Community Baptist Church lived in that complex, and they moved their cell meeting location to his home. The group prayerwalked the complex, organized events for the children there, and subsequently had opportunity to reach the parents. Within one year, they planted four new cells in that complex.

3. Believers Plant a Satellite Cell.

Sometimes a cell member is part of a community quite different from his or her regular cell group. Examples include college students and armed forces personnel. No other cell members are able to join in reaching this community. In fact, there may be no one else in the whole church who is part of the unreached group. In this scenario, the believer teams up with Christians from other churches to launch a prayer point within the targeted neighborhood or community or subgroup. The interchurch prayer group gets a foot inside the door to establish a witness for Christ there.

This strategy is effective with transitional communities, such as youth and military groups, that have a limited length of time together. These kinds of groups call for pioneering methods, because if the body of Christ doesn't reach people quickly they will soon be gone. At the same time, new people enter the community regularly and require fresh outreach. FCBC started its satellite cell ministry in the armed forces, with a vision to plant a cell in every army camp in Singapore.

The satellite cell strategy also works well in office buildings. The initial prayer group may meet during the lunch hour to intercede for the salvation of colleagues. In this kind of setting, a full-fledged cell will not likely be possible. Group members may do two out of the Four W's in a given week, perhaps others a different week. We encourage satellite cell leaders to use cell principles but stay flexible. As the prayer group becomes known, the unsaved will often come and ask for prayer and begin to see God at work.

Because satellite cells are transitional, they must be attached to a parent cell via the FCBC member or members who participate in both the satellite and the parent cell. The satellite cannot operate fully as an FCBC cell because it includes believers from other churches. Nevertheless, FCBC will provide leadership if one of its members rallies the initial prayer point. New converts in the satellite may join the church of their choice.

Some satellite cells grow to include all Four W's as well as the program and functions of a full cell. If the cell continues to grow, it may even multiply to create a new group. If there are now enough FCBC members to form a group of their own, we then consider this a full cell under our vision and leadership. In this way we assure that the cell members receive our full package of equipping and training opportunities as well as the vision for future growth and outreach.

COMMON TARGETS: WHERE SHOULD WE PLANT A CELL?

In reaching out to plant cells where none currently exist, we are seeking fresh nutrients for the growth of our current body of cells, to reference the analogy with biological cells. We look for new environments and new contacts that have not been exhausted by previous evangelistic efforts. As we pray, the Lord reveals groups that still need a Christian community among them to incarnate the love of Jesus.

There are at least three kinds of homogeneous target groups appropriate for cell planting. These groups have something in common that binds them together.

1. Common Location

In this case, the location provides the common ground for the target group. A cell-planting effort may aim to reach a particular housing complex, neighborhood, office building, school, army camp, or other geographic territory.

2. Common Function

A cell-planting effort may also target people with a common function. People who work in the same profession or industry—nurses, politicians, taxi drivers, artists, or musicians, for example—will often respond to outreach tailored to meet their needs. Some efforts may even aim at subgroups with more than one link, such as industrial workers who are first-generation immigrants. In other cases, the function and location will overlap, as when targeting a particular hospital or factory.

3. Common Needs or Interests

Common needs or interests also link people together. Cell planters may see a need for a cell among latchkey kids, the aged, the deaf, the disabled, enthusiasts of a particular sport or hobby, single parents, newly-weds, or cancer patients, for instance. Through FCBC's Touch Community Services arm, the Singaporean government actually pays us to lead support groups for people needing marital or premarital counseling.

Groups of all these kinds need cells designed especially for them. We want to make sure every segment of the community has a cell within reach, where people will feel comfortable attending.

CRITICAL STEPS TO TAKE IN PLANTING A CELL

As each cell group considers its call to plant new cells and begins to mobilize for the work, the cell group members must keep several key steps in mind.

1. Pray and Discern the Time.

Cell planting needs revelation from God. It is not simply a program that can be put into place—although basic tools, training, and information provide practical help. To pioneer new cells, we must hear from God as to how and when to use these tools, because every situation is different. The Lord will speak to us and reveal the needs and the receptivity of people's hearts as we penetrate the community by walking, praying, and serving there.

2. Prepare a Core Group.

The parent cell should look for people with kindred spirits who have a shared burden for reaching the unreached. This core group may include believers from other churches. Cell planting should be done by a team, not individuals.

3. Promote a Vision.

It is crucial for the cell-planting team to develop a vision, right from the start, of what God wants them to do. Concerted corporate prayer will bring the vision into focus and develop unity of purpose.

4. Plant a Cell.

When God has given direction and timing, the team plants a cell. This may be a regular or satellite group, depending on the situation. Because satellites are not full-fledged cells, the team must keep in mind the ultimate objective of developing full cell groups that will focus on the vision, follow the cell agenda with the Four W's, and equip their people for ministry.

5. Provide for Pastoral Leadership.

Cell planters will find pastoral leadership crucial to the success of their efforts. Zone pastors work with the team to give guidance and encouragement, as well as provide needed resources. District pastors are mobilized to discern what God is saying about neighborhoods and target groups that need cells planted in their midst and what strongholds might be hindering the advance of the gospel.

6. Preserve the Parent Cell Relationship.

Cell planters keep in close touch with their parent cell, reporting on their progress. The parent cell provides accountability and prayer support to the cell-planting team.

CROSS-CULTURAL MISSIONS

Cell planting is pioneering work. As such, it requires flexibility to handle a variety of new and unexpected situations. The apostle Paul described such an approach in 1 Corinthians 9:19–23: "Though I am free and belong to no man, I make myself a slave to everyone, to win as many as possible. To the Jews I became like a Jew, to win the Jews. To those under the law I became like one under the law (though I myself am not under the law), so as to win those under the law. To those not having the law I became like one not having the law (though I am not free from God's law but am under Christ's law), so as to win those not having the law. To the weak I became weak, to win the weak. I have become all things to all men so that by all possible means I might save some. I do all this for the sake of the gospel, that I may share in its blessings."

This passage illustrates the essence of an incarnational ministry. When reaching out to the lost, we cannot expect them to come to us or become part of us. We must go to them and meet them wherever they are. If they speak Chinese, we must speak Chinese. If they live in one-room flats, we must go there and spend time among them. But if they are wealthy, we don't invite them to a one-room flat for a cell meeting; we find businesspeople with posh places to open their homes. We must become all things to all people.

Whenever we cross cultural boundaries to extend the gospel of Jesus Christ, we engage in missions. Evangelism, whether type "A" or type "B", ordinarily takes place within one's own culture. But many cultures do not have a living witness of Jesus Christ within their midst. For the gospel to reach them, someone outside the culture has to make a deliberate effort to penetrate those barriers and connect with people on the other side. This is the essence of missions.

The cell church must have a vision beyond its own culture. Otherwise, the growth and extension of the kingdom of God will stop at the edge of the community of people who are like the church. In most cities, this limit means the church will not even reach everyone in its own area.

Almost all cities have subcultures distinct from the majority. These cultures may differ according to race or ethnicity, age, social class, education, occupation, or other variables. Cross-cultural missions starts the moment a church catches a vision for these people and sends a team to plant a cell among them. A church with this kind of missions experience on its doorstep will then find its vision expanded for planting whole churches among unreached peoples in other parts of the nation or world.

The cell church is designed to multiply. The growth that begins in the cell groups moves on to the zones and the districts, and even the whole church itself. Just as cells plant other cells, so cell churches should plant other churches.

FCBC's Experience

Faith Community Baptist Church has caught a vision for cross-cultural ministry. We want to plant churches across Asia and beyond. We are still learning how to deal with cultural issues, and in our zeal and limited experience we have made some major mistakes. Some missionaries launch out ready to die for Jesus, but they end up "dying" in other ways because of the ignorance of the sending church. I believe churches have their own role in commissioning church-planting teams, because many parachurch missionaries have minimal training in what is required to pastor and lead a growing church. But we are now partnering more closely with experienced mission agencies, learning from them, and working with them in unity. We have even developed a fraternity of like-minded churches to cooperate in the church-planting process, including smaller cell churches that would not be able to send out missionaries on their own. By whatever means possible, FCBC is committed to training and mobilizing our people to go to the mission field as church planters. And alongside the mistakes, we have seen significant progress.

We try to have an annual missions conference to stimulate missions consciousness. We also have a program of Weekend Mission Exposure for cells, in which a cell can go for a weekend to a house on the nearby island of Batam, Indonesia. Over those two days we talk about the task of world missions, the concept of hidden or unreached people groups, how an individual and a local body can recognize God's call, and that any Christian can and should get involved in missions at some level. We want to create world Christians—that is, people who carry the vision and the need of the lost world in their hearts.

Other programs we have used include Operation Barnabas and the Year of Mobilization. Over a four-year period we sent out more than 100 teams around the world to help transitioning cell churches in other cultures. Because all of these team members had completed our Year of Equipping (detailed in the next chapter), they knew how to lead and plant cells, how to cast out demons and release the presence of God. In many cases these teams made a tremendous impact and enabled the church to go forward in the transitioning process.

We require each of our missionary candidates to have served in leadership at FCBC, at least as a cell leader, if not a zone supervisor or higher level position. We give candidates psychological testing as well as intense training with monthly meetings, field study, and missions prayer gatherings. Then when we send them out, we ask for an initial commitment of four years. Our rationale is that most people take about two years just to become conversational in their new language. During this time we try to take off the pressure to produce results by calling them "missionaries in training." Afterwards they will be able to take more active steps toward planting a cell church in the new culture.

In addition to equipping our own people, we have WorldCells International (WCI) as a way of linking apostolic leaders from around the world who want to partner together in planting cell churches. The main focus God has given us initially is Central Asia, then beyond to all of Asia. Our eventual goal is to plant cell group churches in each nation of the 10/40 Window, the most spiritually needy region of the world.

Crossing Cultural Barriers Locally

Missions vision starts locally. Before sending church-planting teams across the world, a church should begin by planting a church cross-culturally in its own backyard. One FCBC cell group experienced this firsthand when the Lord intervened powerfully in answer to a specific prayer.

A team from this cell group went to a hospital to visit the sick, encourage people, and pray as requested. One woman they met had had a foot amputated three months earlier because of diabetes. Complications had kept her hospitalized, and the team learned that the woman's husband and only daughter had never visited her during the three months since her surgery. Can you imagine? Probably the husband's irresponsibility rose from his inability to cope emotionally with the fact that his wife had lost a foot. Rather than facing up to it, he ran from reality, like a lot of men.

This poor woman suffered not only the loss of her foot, but also the sense of rejection from her family. As the team visited with her, they felt led to pray with her specifically that the Lord would change her husband's heart and that she would get to see him within the week. They prayed with confidence as the Lord gave them great faith.

Their prayer took place on a Sunday. By Monday morning, the woman's husband showed up with their young daughter. What a glorious answer to prayer! Only Christians who don't believe in the power of God would say this was a coincidence. The unsaved would immediately recognize God's intervention. And during the team's next visit to the hospital, the woman gave her life to Jesus.

Now the team had a responsibility to disciple her. It turned out she lived in a one-room flat in a Mandarin-speaking community. This kind of home consists of essentially four walls in which a family does everything—eats, sleeps, even bathes in the corner bathroom. It sounds better if you call it a studio apartment. But sometimes a family of six or eight people will live there in the one room.

The team told their cell about this woman's situation, and when she was released from the hospital the whole cell decided to plant a new cell in her one-room flat. They also decided to speak Mandarin in this new cell in order to attract the people in the woman's cultural milieu. Most Chinese in Singapore, although educated in English, know some Mandarin. So with their broken Mandarin they went in and started a cell group in this woman's home, joining her culture and speaking her language. Over the next few months, her husband and several other people came to know the Lord.

This new cell was a missionary cell plant, because the cell members crossed cultural boundaries to reach people who needed the love of Jesus Christ. They made sure the cell environment was comfortable and accessible to the woman's family members and their friends and neighbors. Planting this kind of missionary cell means that when the cell grows big enough to multiply, with trained cell interns now ready to lead, the new cells will consist of people within that culture. One or two people from the original planting cell might remain as missionaries to the new groups, but most of the original cell members can then withdraw and look for their next opportunity to plant a cell cross-culturally.

Following Our Father's Example

What a great way for ordinary church members to become missionaries! Cross-cultural opportunities for cell planting abound in most cities of any size. As we allow God to use us in such situations, our hearts will expand for unreached people even further removed from hearing the life-giving gospel of Jesus. This burden will mobilize us to go to needy areas and plant new churches that can in turn grow and multiply.

Only a missionary vision will keep cells and churches from stagnating when they have exhausted their own cultural networks. Planting new cells and churches keeps life flowing through the sending bodies as they direct their efforts toward the growth of the new offshoots. First of all, however, God needs to change our hearts, because a missionary vision calls for a greater commitment. It requires greater faith, greater love, and greater effort than just conveniently inviting our friends to a cell group. But we have no choice if we are to obey God, because the heart of the Lord is to win the lost, to search relentlessly for the 100th wandering sheep and bring it into the fold (see Luke 15:3–7).

As pioneer missionary Henry Martyn said, "The Spirit of Christ is the spirit of missions, and the nearer we get to Him the more intensely missionary we must become." After all, God Himself sent His only Son cross-culturally as a missionary to a lost world. If we want to be like Him, we dare not fail to follow His example.

Nine

Releasing God's People:

— *Equipping in the Cell Church* —

The perpetual-motion machine has enticed inventors as a kind of "holy grail" for hundreds of years. The Renaissance genius Leonardo da Vinci made a number of drawings of proposed mechanisms. The vision of a device that produces more energy than is supplied to it has captivated the minds of many who have spent lives and fortunes in quest of the dream. By the early 1900s, some 600 patents had been granted for supposed perpetual-motion machines. The problem? None of them worked!

No doubt such a useful device would revolutionize modern civilization. Reputable scientists, however, believe a perpetual-motion machine is a physical impossibility that violates the laws of thermodynamics. Nevertheless, numerous inventors, both sincere and crack-pot, continue to claim they have found the secret of free energy. The United States patent office, in despair, has resorted to issuing this notice: "The Office hesitates to accept fees from applicants who believe they have discovered Perpetual Motion, and deems it only fair to give such applicants a word of warning that fees cannot be recovered after the case has been considered by the Examiner."

Endless pages of drawings, diagrams, and descriptions cannot produce perpetual motion without a working model that demonstrates real-life attainment of the vision. The same principle holds for such ideas as the cell church. In this chapter I will show how to begin converting the broad concepts of the cell church into reality. A great theory that does not translate into a concrete, functional plan remains only a theory. We need specific strategies to make the idea work for everyone.

The key to raising up a successful cell church, or transitioning to that model, lies in the equipping process. The cell church structure depends on effective training and nurture of a body of believers who are growing in spiritual maturity and gifting. The church must be able to put into the hands of its people the equipment they need to fulfill their roles in achieving the corporate vision of the church.

Equipping involves practical application. Telling people what they must do by teaching concepts cannot compare to training them how to accomplish specific goals. A track coach cannot train pole-vaulters by lecturing out of a textbook. He must get onto the field and demonstrate the techniques personally, then release his team members to step out and try vaulting themselves under his supervision. The same process holds in the kingdom of God. Equipping is the core of discipleship.

In many traditional churches, equipping takes place in a sporadic and sometimes haphazard fashion. When the Lord puts a burden for prayer on the church's agenda, for example, we might develop a sermon series, write a curriculum, and organize a seminar. Then when a good speaker on prayer comes to town we will invite that person to address our people. Several seminars later, however, people discover they are too busy attending seminars to practice what they have been taught.

The cell church calls for a change from sporadic classes to systematic equipping. In Faith Community Baptist Church, we have developed a system focused on the desired end result—a growing community of Christians with common training that gives them the skills and equipment to carry out vibrant and ongoing ministry. While it is possible to overdo systematizing, we ask the Holy Spirit to baptize us with His power and presence so that He fleshes out the skeleton structure in ways appropriate to each member.

Experiential Learning for Value Change

One of the biggest challenges faced when transitioning into a cell church comes from people who think the structure produces "shallow" Christians who get released into ministry too soon. Often such people are used to content-heavy Bible teaching. Unfortunately, however, people with this kind of training all too often build up their layers of knowledge without corresponding lifestyle application. God needs to change our mindsets to show us that truth is not truly learned until we live it. Being able to pass a theological exam makes no difference unless the truth has become real in our lives.

What, then, is "depth" or "shallowness" in the Christian life? I define depth as a core understanding that personal experience of God's truth is what changes the hearts of people toward loving the Lord their God with all of their being. In chapter 3 I discussed the three domains of learning—the cognitive, the psychomotor, and the affective domains. All three are important but individually limited. We need more of a balance among them than the traditional church structure has provided. The affective domain, often neglected, is the realm in which people's values change based on experiential learning through community life. Thus the cell itself provides an environment where this kind of change takes place. People catch fire for particular concepts by being in a community where others are enthusiastically putting those concepts into practice.

Most of us "experience" theology before we truly understand it. The events of Pentecost after Jesus' ascension bear out this principle. I am arguing not for experience-centered theology, but for experience-tested theology. Our beliefs and theological paradigms must be experienced in real life, or they remain as little more than head knowledge. We need more occasions when the things we are learning touch our hearts and transform us. And to grow as a successful cell church, we must provide opportunities to build into the lives of believers a core set of experiences in which value change can and does happen.

A MEDICAL SCHOOL AND A MILITARY ACADEMY

For this reason, I pattern our equipping process after that of a medical school. Physician interns not only study under their medical school professors, they also receive hands-on training from skilled doctors in various fields. I would hesitate to receive treatment from a doctor who had passed all the exams but never had any practical training experience with live patients! Likewise, someone who learns how to pastor a church from seminary professors—who may never have pastored a church themselves—will be severely disadvantaged. We need to learn ministry skills from people who have exercised these skills successfully themselves, who can model them for us and then coach us as we learn from experience by doing them ourselves.

Our equipping process is also like a military academy. No matter where someone will serve—Army, Navy, Air Force, combat or support—everyone goes through the same basic training in boot camp. Basic training provides everyone with a common language and nomenclature, common community values, and common skill in how to use the equipment correctly. When the commanders know that every recruit has experienced the same training in boot camp, they can take troops to the field, give commands, and make the right decisions in confidence that the troops will capably carry out the orders. After boot camp, some may go on to train as officers, specialists, or commandos, but everyone shares the experience of basic training.

Our Year of Equipping is FCBC's equivalent of basic training. It provides everyone in the church with a common, hands-on learning experience.

The Year of Equipping

Faith Community Baptist Church defines the Year of Equipping as our centralized spiritual boot camp. It has two purposes: to incorporate every member into the family of God at FCBC, and to equip each of them for spiritual ministry. During this period (which may last shorter or longer than a year, depending on an individual's schedule), we encourage people to try different kinds of ministries and gain a basic understanding of each. This enables people to discover what ministries best suit them before they begin to focus on a particular "specialty."

The conceptual framework for the Year of Equipping comes from 1 John 2:12–13 (NKJV): "I write to you, little children, because your sins are forgiven you for His name's sake. I write to you, fathers, because you have known Him who is from the beginning. I write to you, young men, because you have overcome the wicked one. I write to you, little children, because you have known the Father."

In this passage we recognize three categories of Christians: "little children," "young men," and "fathers." "Little children" describes those brand-new in the faith, as well as those who have a new Christian's maturity level because of personal issues. The one main thing they know is that their sins have been forgiven by God. (We define longer-term Christians with chronic issues as "broken wings," and have set up for them a counseling ministry with support groups so that they do not overburden their regular cell groups.) "Young men" include those men and women of all ages who are learning to wrestle and have victory in their Christian lives, and are prepared to share the gospel with those still in Satan's kingdom. In most cases these growing believers still have many contacts with unbelievers from their oikos networks and can win them to Christ readily. "Fathers" are the spiritual fathers and mothers who have led others to Christ and learned to be responsible parents for them—that is, mature believers who have both birthed and raised spiritual children, including type "B" non-believers.

The equipping structure at FCBC makes sure that all three categories of Christians fellowship together in the cell groups. The Year of Equipping aims to help "little children" (including "broken wings") become "young men" and "young men" become "fathers." Progressive growth continues until their lives become productive and fruitful, setting the stage for a lifetime of learning and development in ministry. Some may move on to become cell leaders or zone supervisors, or may even sense a call to full-time ministry. Others find a specialty calling as prayer warriors, church planters, mission mobilizers, and so on.

The Core Curriculum

The core curriculum of the Year of Equipping consists of two parts—the inward journey and the outward journey. The curriculum of the inward journey helps people deal with their own strongholds, become overcomers, and grow in the Lord. The curriculum of the outward journey teaches people to become ministers and to help others also grow spiritually.

The Inward Journey

Training in the inward journey deals with the basics of the Christian life and enables the individual to get started in spiritual growth. Topics include prayer, community life, dealing with sin, and knowing the Word of God.

Much of the inward journey training takes place in the context of the cell group. Each incoming cell member is visited by the cell leader, who assigns another member to serve as a sponsor for the new person. The two core resource materials for the inward journey are simple booklets designed to be used in a sponsor–sponsee relationship within the cell group. These booklets are entitled *Beginning Your New Life* and *Living Your New Life*. The choice of material is not as important as connecting the new cell member into a relationship with his or her sponsor.

The sponsor also receives a sponsor's guide for each of these two booklets, containing step-by-step instructions on how to lead the incoming cell member through the materials. Christians who have recently completed this material themselves make excellent sponsors of brand-new believers. For one thing, they relate easily to the new converts and their spiritual issues. Also, serving as a sponsor helps reinforce their own understanding of each weekly lesson and gives them some basic leadership training. The cell leader is always available to help the sponsor in this role and to help the newcomer with anything the sponsor cannot handle.

Faith Community Baptist Church also uses a tool called *Your New Journey Guide*. This booklet, given to the incoming cell member, explains the equipping and discipling process. It includes a questionnaire for the new member to complete, with a section on strongholds. This is used to acquaint the cell leader and sponsor with the spiritual condition of the person. After reading through the completed questionnaire, the sponsor can discuss specific issues with the sponsee in private weekly sessions.

In addition, the inward journey includes a spiritual formation weekend that serves as a membership class for FCBC. The prospective new members receive orientation in the basics of the faith, the cell church concept, and the vision of the church. All those who want to join FCBC—even mature, baptized believers—must attend the spiritual formation weekend training. Holding this seminar on one weekend enables new members to complete the training easily, whereas a weekly membership class that stretches for eight or ten weeks becomes an administrative nightmare when some people miss one or more sessions and have to make up that material. Following the spiritual formation weekend, those who need deliverance or baptism will receive it.

Installing These Resources En Masse

How can a congregation transitioning to the cell church model install the two basic resource materials—*Beginning Your New Life* and *Living Your New Life*—and their accompanying sponsor guides? For a mass installation, the senior pastor should plan to preach a six-sermon series on the six lessons of the initial booklet, with everyone going through the lessons at home. Then, during the Word segment of the cell meetings, people pair up using the sponsor's guide. Cell members take turns from week to week in the sponsor or sponsee role, so that everyone gets experience in sponsoring someone else and becomes prepared to train new believers joining the cell.

After a break of two or three months, the same process is followed for the second booklet. Once the senior pastor has provided this jump start, the equipping process will feed itself through the cells, because the cells will have enough people already trained to incorporate newcomers. In addition, the pastor's taped sermon on each lesson can be given to new cell members with each of the two lesson booklets as reinforcement for the teaching.

The Outward Journey

The curriculum of the outward journey aims to release people into evangelism and ministry. This training is incorporated into the cycles of harvest that occur three times each year. As described in chapter 7, these cycles usually include the two cell-based harvest events at Good Friday and Christmas, plus a large celebration harvest event in August. The cycles of harvest serve as both an equipping process and an engine that helps to make evangelism an ongoing lifestyle.

A complete cycle of harvest includes a weekend training seminar, followed by ten weeks of exposure and practice in the cell groups, culminating in an evangelistic harvest event. Each of these three elements is part of the outward journey equipping curriculum.

Seminars of the outward journey include the weekend type "A" evangelism training and the two-weekend spiritual warfare training (both seminars also described in chapter 7), as well as a weekend orientation on how to be a sponsor. This third seminar trains first-time sponsors to minister to new cell members using the two core booklets, *Beginning Your New Life* and *Living Your New Life*.

Each of these three training seminars is offered three times a year during the cycles of harvest, with a one-month break for assimilation of new members. People who have already taken the type "A" evangelism weekend seminar, for instance, may choose one of the others.

Additional Training

Besides the core curriculum described above as it relates to both the inward journey and the outward journey, the Year of Equipping offers numerous other equipping and discipling resources and activities to supplement the core. Many of these are designed so individuals can work through the material or training activities at home, at their own pace, and in the sequence that most interests them.

FCBC has designed an equipping log so every cell member can track the learning experiences he or she has undertaken. These include completion of the *Beginning Your New Life* booklet, participation in cell group meetings, development of quiet times with the Lord, learning how to read the Bible, and reading specific books of Scripture, among many other equipping experiences. Three times per year the cell members take out their equipping logs and talk about which resources or activities they have recently completed and which ones they plan to pursue in the coming months.

A cell leader named Judy caught the vision for equipping believers in preparation for rapid growth and outreach. Her enthusiasm enabled her to motivate every member of her cell to complete the Year of Equipping quickly. When her cell multiplied in February 1998, one of her cell interns, Sean, took one group and Judy the other. Each of them continued to encourage their new cell members to take advantage of the Year of Equipping curriculum. During the "I'll Be Home for Christmas" harvest event in December 1998, the two cells joined forces to host three outreaches—one for children, one for disabled people, and one for friends and colleagues. Because the cell members had been trained through the Year of Equipping, they each had the skills and the heart-felt desire to share the gospel with pre-Christian cell guests. At those three cell-sponsored outreach events, 18 people gave their lives to the Lord.

DEVELOPING LIFE MINISTRY TRAINING

The training arm of Faith Community Baptist Church is called the TOUCH Equipping Station System, or TESS. As mentioned in chapter 3, we emphasize that each step of the equipping process serves as a station to enable believers to continue their journey toward greater maturity in life and ministry. No station is an end in itself.

TESS consists of five equipping stages. The Year of Equipping, which incorporates the core curriculum, comprises the Basic Christian Growth stage and the Intermediate Christian Growth stage. When members have completed this training, they may be challenged to move on to the Christian Servanthood stage for leadership training. This process raises up new cell leaders.

As each new cell begins, the cell leader identifies at least one intern to be trained as a prospective group leader when the cell multiplies. Over a several-month period, the cell leader begins to pass responsibility to the intern, so that by two or three months before the cell multiplies, the intern is actually leading the group. In this way the intern acquires both practical skills and leadership authority, so people will be willing to follow him or her when a new group forms. Concurrent with this "on-the-job" mentoring, newly identified interns and their spouses receive nine weeks of training from their zone pastor in a cell group format. In this setting the zone pastor can evaluate each intern's suitability and readiness for leadership. The zone pastor uses a well-developed instructor's manual and each intern receives a trainee's manual. While zone pastors may teach additional material adapted to the needs of the group, they may not skip sections, because the manual assures a level of quality control and gives our cell leaders a common core of training.

A similar internship program raises up zone supervisors, using both a trainer's manual and a trainee's workbook.

Besides the Christian Servanthood stage, members may be encouraged to advance to the Specialized Christian Ministry stage that equips people for specific ministry in accordance with their calling and giftings. We also offer the Continuous Christian Growth stage to provide members with ongoing and lifetime ministry training.

EQUIPPING FOR ALL

Equipping is not meant for adults only. Virtually all the materials and training experiences we have developed for adults come in children's versions as well. For instance, we have a *Children's Journey Guide,* and a packet with the John 3:16 presentation in sticker form. Our goal is to equip parents to train their own children in spiritual maturity using these materials. Children may even ask their parents to talk about their own Christian walk, prompting growth in the parents. A 50-week "family cell" program enables parents to lead a family devotional time using the same Four W's format as in regular cells—Welcome, Worship, Works, and Word. This program, based on a book by Dr. Lorna Jenkins called *The Family Journeys Together,* is adaptable for use with children of different ages. In the process, the parents receive reinforcement in learning as they teach their children. Then the children themselves can use this same material to disciple other kids. We also have resources for children whose parents have not yet come to Christ.

For people who sense a calling to full-time ministry, FCBC offers the TESS Training School to raise up zone pastors. This 18-month program, recognized by the Wagner Leadership Institute, involves both classroom instruction and practical training. Students attend classes in the morning for the first 12 months. Concurrently for 18 months, they undergo a carefully designed internship under the supervision of an experienced zone pastor. The trainees progress from being cell members to co-leading cells to observing and emulating a zone pastor at work. As with the other equipping programs, the TESS Training School can serve as a model for people in other countries who want to set up their own programs.

In addition to an annual International Conference on Cell Group Churches each spring, FCBC also offers a follow-up intensive course for senior pastors and key pastors. The TESS Intensive lasts two and a half weeks each September, and includes scheduled hands-on events such as the two-weekend spiritual warfare training seminar.

Through years of experience and observation, I strongly urge churches who want to implement cell church principles and programs to try the full package for two years before adapting the model. We have found that the parts of the structure are well integrated, and the implementation and success of one part may depend on the implementation and success of another. After a two-year trial, a church will more fully understand the cell church model and have a better perspective on what items should be adapted to its unique situation. Of course, it is vital for each church to develop and teach its own vision statement.

I am delighted to hear when churches come up with their own ideas and materials that best accomplish their goals, because I myself want to continue learning and refining what works. My ongoing prayer is that churches partner together to enable the body of Christ by all means to evangelize the world as soon as possible.

Training of cell members for both growth and outreach provides the backbone for the cell church. Through this structure the church disciples people in their own spiritual journeys and releases them into leadership service at all levels. As we implement these strategies, the Holy Spirit brings to reality the vision of our divine calling in Ephesians 4:12 (NKJV): "the equipping of the saints for the work of ministry."

Ten

RENEWING THE WINESKIN:

— Transitioning to the Cell Church —

Children love fairy tales. Truth be told, adults often love them, too! In one brief story a terrible problem gets solved, the hero saves the day, and good triumphs over evil. Usually all it takes to bring instant transformation is knowing the secret word, finding the hidden key, or drinking the enchanted potion. In no time at all, love blooms, the comatose awaken, and frogs become princes. And, of course, everyone lives happily ever after.

The story of how Faith Community Baptist Church transitioned to become a cell church is a real-life story, not a fairy tale. We did not discover any instant answers. We did not push a button or kiss a frog or say any magic words that would turn our congregation overnight into a successful, smoothly functioning cell church. The transitioning process required a lot of time and hard work. We experimented, made mistakes, and tried to learn from them. In fact, even when FCBC was running completely according to the cell model, we had to keep refining our processes. Still today we continue checking and working on our methods and procedures, because every system starts to atrophy over time. Even the best systems fall apart eventually, because we live in a fallen-apart world. There are no fairy-tale solutions.

At the same time, I believe that churches approaching the

transitioning process today will have an easier time and make the change more quickly than we did. I sense the Lord building an environment around the world in which there is greater acceptance of the cell ministry. It doesn't matter whether it reflects FCBC style or some other form. An atmosphere of openness now allows the Holy Spirit greater freedom to work through the cell model. In addition, more materials and resources are readily available, and more churches that have made the transition can encourage and advise others.

Our experience at FCBC should prove instructive as well as motivating for many who are ready to consider transitioning to a cell church. Let's take a look at it.

GROUP LIFE DYNAMICS

At Faith Community Baptist Church, we use a graph that shows the typical process of group life dynamics through the approximately 12-month life cycle of a cell group, from birth to reproduction. What's interesting is that we have seen the entire church going through the same four stages during our transitioning history.

At the start of a new group, members go through a "get acquainted" period. This stage often feels awkward, as people begin to relate to others they don't know yet. Everyone wants to make a good impression. Group members need time to learn to trust each other, and may guard themselves until they do.

In the next stage, people who have learned to trust begin opening up. As they feel accepted by the group, they allow others to see more of who they are, warts and all. As a result, the group enters a "conflict/worship" period. The conflict stage is actually a sign of progress and growth, because brand-new groups are not close enough to fight. Only after we have come to know people and established relationships do we begin to express irritation or criticism. The closer we are, the more we get in each other's way.

While we should not allow conflict to spiral out of control, we need not despair when we sense discord arising. It means the group is maturing and has opportunity to grow further. The best solution to conflict, whether in a cell group or in a whole church, is to focus on the Lord. Hashing things out directly does not always settle the problem. Indeed, some issues may defy resolution. But when we look to the Lord, both individually and corporately, our attitudes change. That's why we call this the "conflict/worship" stage. Worship helps us push through conflict to reach higher levels in our group life dynamics.

Following this stage, the group enters the "community" period. Now group members feel like family. Interpersonal ties stabilize and strengthen. The life of the group continues to build.

Finally, the fourth stage of group life dynamics is the "multiplication" period. The group, strong and growing, begins to plan for the birth of a new group. One group becomes two, and the cycle of group dynamics begins again.

Although Faith Community Baptist Church held its first service in August 1986, it was not until early 1987 that we started getting settled as to our identity and purpose. During this vision-forming and vision-clarifying stage, I met often with my leadership team. We asked questions, discussed, and crystallized what God was saying to us. That season of wrestling produced the three-part vision described in chapter 4.

LAUNCHING THE CELL CHURCH

After Ralph Neighbour opened my eyes to the cell church model, I started preparing FCBC for a cell group launch. The process was not simple, because FCBC already had about 1,200 members. Some pastors seem to feel that a tiny church of 40 or 50 people presents more difficulties, but the opposite is true. Transitioning a large church requires much greater effort. FCBC certainly did not have everything going for it as it made the change.

Before transition, FCBC had at least 20 Bible study groups, many of which I led personally. These were high-level groups for people earnestly pursuing more of Jesus. Sometimes when people came and asked, "Could I have a Bible study with you?" I would say, "Great! I'll see you at 5:30 tomorrow morning!" Their response told me whether they were really serious about studying the Word of God. Some of my department heads came out of those groups.

These studies centered around the Bible. We went deep into the Word and memorized verses, often using Navigators and Campus Crusade for Christ materials. My seminary background fed this orientation.

But something I learned from one of my professors in expository preaching stuck with me. He said, "Lawrence, don't preach the Bible. Preach lives. Preach people. But make sure everything you say comes from the Bible." After I returned to Singapore following seminary graduation, I gradually tried putting this concept into practice. My pulpit ministry started with a foundation in the Bible and then jumped into people's lives. My sermons did not just skim the surface but focused on down-to-earth issues. I saw that when my preaching touched sensitive areas, I got a response. And when listeners said "ouch," their lives began to change.

Learning this lesson freed me from the worry that my teaching was not deep enough into the Bible. In turn, I began to let go of the notion that small groups should always have in-depth study of Scripture as their primary focus. So when I heard about the cell church model, with its focus on intimate small groups that stressed worship, prayer, and outreach in addition to Bible study, I was ready to dive into it. But first I had to sell the idea to my leadership.

Leading a Cell Group

As an initial step, I set out to lead a cell group myself. I recruited two of my leaders, Melvyn Mak and Eugene Seow, to join the group as my understudies so they would be prepared to take over and lead new groups when the first one multiplied. We filled the cell with believers from outside the leadership team to demonstrate that all Christians, not just spiritual giants, belonged in cells.

The cell grew in both maturity and numbers as God blessed it. And while that first cell group differed in many ways from the cell format we currently use, it gave me a basic understanding of some of the dynamics involved in how a cell works and how to lead one.

Convincing the Leaders

While I led this cell, I began talking with my leadership team, including the leaders of the Bible studies then in progress. Morning by morning I went around from group to group, sharing with them about the cell church and convincing them this model could serve as the strategy to fulfill our corporate vision of reaching the lost. We talked for hours. I met with people one on one as well as in groups.

After two or three months, about 90 percent of my leaders were ready to say, "Pastor, let's give it a try. I believe in it." Meanwhile, half of the remaining ten percent told me, "Pastor, I'm not sure. I'm hearing you, but the idea gives me butterflies. I'm nervous about it." In response to these people, I asked them, "Do you trust me? We've been friends for years now. Would I lead you down a road if I were not convinced about it? Just trust me, OK?" These folks then got on board.

Then perhaps five percent had a different reaction. "Pastor, I could follow you just because I love you, but it would go against what I feel is right." To these folks I responded, "I know how difficult it is to do something you feel uncomfortable about. Why don't I set you free from being a group leader? You don't have to leave the church. Stay in the group and I'll find someone to replace you as leader, or else we'll just close your group and find something else."

A few of these people decided to continue as group leaders, but they never did change their Bible study group into a cell. When I perceived this, I had to bury some of these groups a couple of years later, with tears and regret. Over time, however, we moved closer to the model of a cell church.

Training Cell Leaders

Today churches transitioning to the cell church have many more resources and materials available than Faith Community Baptist Church did in 1987 and 1988. Just about all we had was Ralph Neighbour's manual for cell leaders, *The Shepherd's Guidebook*. Sometimes I as senior pastor felt a little like the blind leading the blind, except that a vision consumed me and I could see with faith the end result.

We used *The Shepherd's Guidebook* and also began to write our own materials, expanding our inventory of resources over the next several years. In this way we trained and prepared about 20 new cell group leaders. By this time, too, the cell group I had begun had multiplied and spawned new groups.

Finally, in May 1988 we felt ready for launch. I preached for two or three Sundays on the cell church, and then exhorted all the church members to sign up for a cell group. Out of a congregation of 1,200 people, about 300 or 400 responded to the initial call. I was pleased with this result.

That week, every cell group was packed with people. A month later, however, most of them had dropped out. Why? Maybe the cell group seemed boring and a little disorganized. Some people thought, "Now it's not a Bible study anymore, but we don't really know what it is."

Still, we kept pressing on and trying different approaches, all the while with our vision firmly in mind. From 1988 to 1991 I had to do a new cell group launch every year, taking a few weekends to preach on the concept again.

In 1989 one cell group multiplied twice, resulting in a total of four groups in the second generation. I was so excited that I used this group as a sermon illustration. I had the original group members stand on the stage and demonstrate who joined them, who became the new cell leaders, who joined the new groups, and so on. Starting with six or eight people, the stage soon filled with people. The whole church rejoiced. But that was our only such example.

Many of the other cell groups died—or carried on in a kind of suspended animation, neither growing nor dying. During this difficult period, we simply pressed on in the spirit with eyes of faith. I took encouragement from the confidence of Elijah in 1 Kings 18:41–46, when he saw a small, hand-sized cloud and declared the imminent arrival of a mighty rainstorm to a land parched with drought.

PUTTING IN THE CELL STRUCTURE

Between 1988 and 1991, most of my leadership made their own mental transition and bought into the cell concept. We kept working to develop cell life. At that time, the cell agenda of the Four W's (Welcome, Worship, Works, and Word) began to emerge. As we tried to solidify this, we continued to exhort leaders to multiply the cell groups. Some did and some did not. But in those early days, multiplication did not involve much outside evangelism, because many church members did not yet belong to a cell. Cells grew relatively easily as people invited others from the worship service to join a group.

As more groups started, we needed to train more cell leaders and initiate training of zone supervisors. I discovered that I trained zone supervisors too slowly. I held onto Ralph Neighbour's ideal that a cell leader should multiply a group twice before he or she becomes a zone supervisor. But as cell groups began to multiply more rapidly, I found that I did not yet have that level of leadership. In order to raise up more zone supervisors to keep a closer connection between the cell leaders and the zone pastors, I sometimes actually had to close a cell group to tap its leader as a zone supervisor.

This was difficult for both the group and the leader. The cell leader, already responsible for training an intern for the next group, now also faced the need to get someone to take over in his or her own place. On these occasions I had to go to the group and say, "God has called your cell leader to be a zone supervisor, and you are going to have to make a great sacrifice. To free up your leader, why don't we merge you with another cell? After you merge, you're going to multiply in three months' time." By raising up new zone supervisors, we provided a connectivity to the grass roots.

During this period, FCBC grew from 1,200 to about 2,000 members. It was a scary time. God had anointed me in the pulpit, in addition to anointing our worship leaders, and people came to church because they were attracted to that—but I wondered if the cell growth could possibly catch up. Thanks be to God, it finally did. By about 1991, almost everyone in FCBC was part of a cell. One exciting reason for this came in 1991 with a visitation of the Holy Spirit. People who had been sitting on the fence saw the power of the Lord, and He clinched the deal. Although this doesn't happen in every transitioning situation, the Lord blessed us with a season of repentance and revival.

POSITIONING FOR GROWTH

From 1991 to 1994, we concentrated on strengthening the training and equipping process. We wanted to systematize it for ease of administration and quality control. Because available resources were limited then, we tackled one thing at a time. We bought books and wrote more books. Sometimes we tried too much, and leaders got weighed down and discouraged by the pace of the introduction of new material and methods. Soon we had a new nickname: "FCBC— Fast Changing Baptist Church"! But we had to change in order to improve and find solutions. Every experimental step helped us learn how to equip and evangelize in the new paradigm. We were determined to discard anything that did not help us achieve our goals, so we revised our strategy again and again as we gained experience. Indeed, we are still doing so!

From 1994 on, the Lord directed us to a particular all-church focus for each year, including missions, mobilization, and so forth. One key to successful leadership involves being able to see one or two years down the road and prepare people ahead of time for what God wants to do. A massive new idea, whether transitioning to the cell church, equipping for cell planting, or any other major concept, generally requires two years of incubation before it becomes reality. People must become convinced of the idea's importance before they will commit to work toward its implementation. So a leader must be able to see what is needed ahead of time and begin to talk about it.

Every idea goes through this incubation period, then growth and fruition, then a time after the idea has crested and played out when it begins to taper off. A leader needs to start thinking and talking about the next step *before* the current idea crests. This way the new development gets incubated in advance of its launch time, and when the current season's focus begins to wane, the people are ready for the next step.

As a leader, I'm not living for this year. For me, this year is history—I'm merely living out what is already finished by faith. I'm thinking about next year and the year after that. Churches transitioning to the cell model must keep these issues of timing in mind in order to plan for rollout of new phases and maintain a realistic assessment of their progress.

TRANSITIONING THE LEADERSHIP: PRINCIPLES

Let's look at some principles involved in the transitioning process that can be applied to any church. As we have seen from the FCBC story, the major portion of the process involves transitioning the leadership. Once the leadership is convinced and ready to say, "Let's go," you have at least half the battle won. Because this is a revolutionary change, not a minor adjustment, you must know that your core leadership is with you. If you go in part way and your leadership begins to balk, you may find you have to start again at square one.

The first phase you will encounter is leadership resistance. Any major new idea will face some opposition, whether great or small. After all, the cell is a whole new way of thinking about church. You as the senior pastor will be calling for a commitment beyond what an average church member is used to. As a result, some fear and resistance will arise. What's interesting is that the greatest resistance will come not from within dying churches. Churches in decline will grab onto any idea that gives them hope. The most opposition will come within large and relatively successful churches—those running an attendance of at least 500 or 1,000 in worship services, with a vital Sunday school program and so on.

When (and if!) leadership resistance breaks down, the next phase is leadership agreement. The church board and leadership core catch the vision for the cell church and agree to move ahead with it. But this step is not enough. You won't be able to complete the transition until you reach the phase of leadership commitment. Your leaders must be so sold on the vision that you can tell your church board, for instance, "Each one of you needs to lead a cell group to get this transition started. If you do not serve as a cell group leader, you will not serve on the board."

Here your leaders will face a real test—and you don't want to put them to this test until they are ready. Don't just threaten them that if they do not lead a cell, or if their cell flops, they will get the axe. You must bring them to a point where they want to do this, because they see that leading a cell is a step in their own growth process. Anyone who wants to be a spiritual leader of a church should surely have enough spiritual influence to lead a cell group successfully. And those who do not should not remain in church leadership simply out of historical precedent. They should step aside and allow into leadership those committed to making the cell vision a reality.

THREE WAYS TO DEAL WITH RESISTANCE

Suppose you want to make the transition to a cell church. There are three ways for a pastor to deal with resistance to this idea.

Resignation

When you approach your leaders with the idea of the cell church, you might hear, "Pastor, you must be joking. We don't need that; it will never work here." The most common response to this kind of resistance is resignation. Of course, most pastors leave on better terms by finding another situation that helps them save face. For example, many pastors in a failing ministry situation decide to go back to school for further studies. That's why too many of our churches are filled with people in ministry who have lots of degrees but no temperature! Pursuing higher education is the most honorable way to get out of a bad situation.

At the same time, resignation is generally the worst solution, because most of the time it indicates a pastor is running away. As pastor, you should resign in the face of resistance only if the Lord tells you to do so. Before then, it is important to use all your wisdom and diplomacy to share your vision so that your leaders can catch it with you. Give the process plenty of time. Then when you have done everything you can and resistance remains, the Lord may release you. But it must be God's choice.

Revolution

The second way to deal with resistance is revolution, when you as senior pastor tell your leadership, in essence, "Do or die. We are going to move toward being a cell church. Either go with the flow or get out of the way."

Revolution is the most painful way to transition, but sometimes it may be a necessary price to pay. You are leading the church into something you have never done before, and you may end up leaving a trail of blood behind. By God's grace, this doesn't have to be so. But in some situations the direct response to resistance proves the best.

Even still, a pastor would do well to give time and diplomacy to the transition. If you yourself needed some time to understand and lay hold of the cell church concept, your leaders will require a similar grace period before they will be ready to embrace it. Proceed step by step and allow time for each phase to take hold.

At the same time, however, if your situation calls for revolution, you will need to lay the bottom line early and not waver from it. If you begin to fudge on your goal by accommodating people with different visions and strategies, you won't arrive at anything. Work toward transition gradually but make sure everyone knows your bottom line.

One mark of a good leader is that when something needs to be dealt with, he or she can wield a sharp and fast knife. If you have a tumor in your body, you don't want the surgeon using a blunt little penknife to jab around here and there. You want the doctor to slash quickly with a sharp scalpel and remove whatever needs to go. After surgery, you may look weak and sickly, with a great loss of blood. But you will be healthier than before, because the tumor is gone and the wound can now heal.

Avoiding confrontation and bad feelings often just drags out a painful process. Leaders who are afraid to wield the knife have an admirable desire to maintain the unity of the body. Too often, however, we have the idea that if nobody is talking about a problem, we have unity. Wrong! If there are two camps divided in opinion that will not budge, then disunity reigns, even if no one is talking about it. The absence of conflict does not mean the presence of unity. It is important to face the problem head-on and not waste each other's time and energy avoiding it.

When it's necessary, just get your knife and move quickly. But don't become a butcher. Don't cut off more than you must. Knowing what parts of your local spiritual body have turned unhealthy requires a skilled judgment call, a skill that may take years to develop.

As I look back on my own experience of being fired by the deacon board of my previous church, I can say that my dismissal was the right decision. Our conflict had dragged on for a year, and neither they nor I wanted to be the bad guy. Meanwhile, bitterness and gossip began festering in the church. When the deacon board came to the conclusion that they had to fire me, everyone was unhappy for a while. But now we can see the Lord's will in the situation. We can carry on and bless each other.

Revolution may be necessary, but be careful how you go about it.

Renewal

The third way to overcome resistance to transition is renewal. If the Holy Spirit touches a body of believers and conveys an unmistakable corporate vision for reaching the lost through the cell church, the body will be able to move together in unity toward the goal. This, of course, is the best solution. But it may also be the most uncommon.

Back in the late 1980s, I remember hearing Dr. C. Peter Wagner speak at an International Church Growth Conference at Pastor David Yonggi Cho's church in Seoul, Korea. Dr. Wagner commented on how many new churches had launched successfully by using the cell model from day one. Then he said, "In my last 15 or 20 years of consultation with churches, I have seen only one established traditional church that succeeded in making a transition to a cell church."

Thank God, this dismal situation has changed. Many churches are succeeding in transition now, because God is doing a new work around the world. He is performing miracles by changing and renewing the old wineskin. It is one thing to see the release of the Spirit's anointing to bless individuals. It is much more of a challenge for the old wineskin to soak in the Spirit long enough to soften, melt, and change. But it is possible, and it has been done. There is hope for churches that want to transition to the cell model through spiritual renewal.

STUDY THE NATURE OF YOUR LEADERS

Senior pastors feeling the call of God toward the cell church model need to become change agents in their churches. A pastor must try to identify and analyze the church's power people—the core leaders, board members, key elders, and other people of influence. After identifying them, the pastor needs to analyze how these people respond to change or new ideas.

The way the individuals in an average group respond to change can be mapped in a bell curve. On the left end are a small number of innovators. These people grasp a new idea and immediately see its benefits. They can visualize the idea bearing fruit even if they have not yet seen it work. I myself am an innovator. I can spot a winner early and pursue it with vigor.

Just to the right of innovators on the bell curve are the early adopters, still a relatively small subgroup. Not quite as visionary as the innovators, they still see and understand new concepts quickly. They will pick up on the fruitful ones with just a few examples of how an idea works in real life. For these people, the senior pastor may need to lead a demonstration cell group for a few months, for instance. Then the early adopters will readily sign on.

Then there is the majority sector called middle adopters, the large portion of the bell curve around the crest. These people do not take the same risks as innovators or early adopters, but after they watch a new idea begin to rise and grow over the first year or two, they will join in and become part of it. Church members who are middle adopters need to see that their pastor is serious about the cell church model and that success looks like a good possibility.

The average group also includes a smaller number of late adopters, those who have to see an idea like the cell church demonstrated for at least two or three years before they decide to jump on the bandwagon. If this category represents most of a church's leaders, the pastor will have some difficulty making the transition to a cell church.

Finally, most groups will have a handful of laggards. These folks shy away from change. Regardless of the demonstrated benefits of a new idea, they often will not accept it until they almost have no other option.

The category characteristic of most of a church's leaders or power people will determine the rate of progress a pastor can expect when implementing the cell church model. If most of a church's leaders are innovators or early adopters, the pastor can plan for a massive launch probably within a year. I praise God that most of my leaders are in these first two categories. About six months after I learned about the cell church, we launched it. The majority of members came on board a little later, but the leadership committed quickly.

In a church where most leaders respond to change as middle adopters, transition could take up to two years before the pastor will be able to launch the concept on a broad basis. Most of this time will be spent with the leaders—sharing, convincing, testing, demonstrating, and so on. With leaders among the late adopters, the process will take even longer. But if most of a church's power people are laggards, I would advise the pastor not even to try convincing them. In such a case the Lord would have to show the pastor whether resignation or revolution would be appropriate.

TRANSITIONING THE LEADERSHIP: PRACTICAL STEPS IN MOBILIZATION

Once you have identified and analyzed the power people of your church and determined the appropriate pace needed for the transitioning process, the next goal is to mobilize these key leaders. Here are some practical steps to take:

1. *Formulate vision and strategy.* I recommend taking your leadership team away on retreat. There you can begin sharing the vision of the cell church, discussing it, and dreaming dreams together.

2. *Study FCBC's conference tapes on cell principles.* To begin, "The New Wineskin" is a 15-minute tape that encapsulates the core issues and enables people to catch the cell church vision. If your leaders watch it and want to know more, full-length tapes from the latest International Conference on Cell Group Churches are available.

3. *Determine the equipping process.* The way you decide to equip your people will govern how you proceed and what you will do with Sunday school classes, for instance.

4. *Determine the organizational chart.* Work with your leaders to begin to draw your dream organizational chart—even though it could take two or three years or longer to achieve. Be sure there is no organizational competition with the cell structure. Cells must not become just another department of the church. You cannot successfully overlay a cell structure on top of an existing structure that includes the usual Sunday school classes, youth and adult fellowships, men's and women's ministries, and so on. To make the transition, some churches may need to run two structures for a while, but if you do not dismantle something soon, the drain on your leadership team will doom your efforts to failure. The cell structure alone is so labor intensive it will demand all available energy and human resources. You must

commit to it and make sure nothing on the organizational chart competes with it.

5. *Select and appoint leaders.* As you begin to draw the organizational chart, ask the Lord how to distribute the present personnel resources to implement the cell structure. Involve every member of the leadership team in this process. If they are willing to move ahead with the vision, make sure each of them becomes part of the cell ministry. In particular, the paid pastoral staff members need to be fully utilized in the cell structure, working toward the job of zone pastor. It's best to distribute them among different zones, even those led by lay leaders, in order to maximize this resource.

When FCBC changed its structure, everyone on my staff led a cell group. As the cells multiplied the leaders became zone supervisors, then zone pastors. For a while the pastoral staff had two jobs—their role in the cell structure and their role as leader of a supporting ministry, such as missions, worship, finances, administration, prayer, counseling, and so on. Some supporting ministries can take a back seat until the cell structure and equipping process are in place. Others must be carried on to keep the church running; additional staff members can help ease the load until the leader has completed a season as zone pastor and raised up others as replacements. Then that leader can focus on the specialized ministry for which he or she is gifted. All my heads of departments in specialized ministries have been zone pastors, so they understand what the cell leaders go through and what it means not to compete with the cells.

6. *Have leaders attend FCBC's annual International Conference on Cell Group Churches.* Although audio- and videotapes are available, coming and soaking in the spiritual environment

provides an experience no tape can duplicate. Conference attenders see for themselves a working cell church. Bringing your leaders also means I can say things to them that they would have difficulty hearing from you as their senior pastor. Defenses get torn down. In fact, some pastors come every year, because they learn new things and it takes time for some ideas to sink in while making the necessary paradigm shifts.

7. *Start a leadership cell.* Select the core leaders who will serve as the initial cell group leaders and start a leadership cell—more than one, if you need more than 10 or 15 initial cell leaders. The best leadership training happens in the context of the cell meeting itself, going through the Four W's and using the training manuals or other available resources. Demonstration, mentoring, and hands-on practice in a small group provide dynamics unavailable in classroom-style training sessions. In addition, begin to walk your core leaders through the Year of Equipping cycle. When your initial leadership cell or cells are ready to multiply, these people will be prepared to reach out and invite others to a cell. You may be able to multiply the initial leadership cell at least three or four ways by pairing up leaders to start new groups.

8. *Start an ordinary cell.* As senior pastor, you need to experience what it is like to lead a group of average Christians who are not ready to consider dying for Jesus, but just want to get the most out of their spiritual lives. As you share your own life with them, they will ask some of the most refreshing questions. Take the challenge of working with them. This kind of experience keeps pastors in touch and enables us to stay real.

9. *Maintain personal interaction with your leaders.* Nothing substitutes for spending plenty of time with your leadership team.

When we first started the cell ministry at FCBC, every cell leader met with his or her zone supervisor and zone pastor every Sunday. With FCBC's growth, we now find this impossible. But we still aim for as much interaction as possible. Many leaders meet for lunch weekly. Connections between leaders on the different levels of the cell structure must stay strong for the structure itself to remain vital.

OVERCOMING OPPOSITION

If you have made the decision to transition to a cell church, you will face some opposition at different points of the process, even if most of your leaders stand with you. How do you deal with it?

1. *Guard the relationship and walk the second mile.* Visit and talk with those who oppose you. Give them time. When you feel like giving up, say to them, "Let's talk again." God willing, they will come to see your point of view. But even if they do not, they will find it hard to stay angry with you if you have walked the second mile to try to reach them. Don't compromise your bottom line to try to make peace, but your willingness to spend time hearing their concerns or hurts will make a huge difference.

2. *Never lose your temper.* Learn to stay cool in the face of opposition. "Everyone should be quick to listen, slow to speak and slow to become angry, for man's anger does not bring about the righteous life that God desires" (James 1:19–20). "A gentle answer turns away wrath" (Proverbs 15:1).

3. *Move with the movers.* Go with those who want to go with you. Spend time around people who encourage you. Pastors are easy targets for people slinging objections or criticism. Sometimes we need to hear what they have to say, but too much input exclusively

from critics will feed discouragement. At my church, for instance, the secretary who screens my mail has a rule that any anonymous "poison letters" will not be forwarded to me. If someone signs a name, at least I can dialog with the person.

4. *Remember, you will never be out of a job!* Stay confident—the Lord has need of you no matter where you are employed. Many of us operate out of fear when it comes to trying something new, because we were never taught how to do anything except maintenance of ongoing ministries. Fear keeps too many pastors from attempting anything that might garner opposition. Remember, if you lost your job tomorrow, you would not walk away with nothing. You would still have your years of experience with the Lord and your willingness to enter into ventures of faith at His direction. As long as you remain usable to God, no person or group or organization can keep you from fulfilling His purposes. You will always have something to do. This assurance does not promote arrogance but affords dignity, courage, and stability.

TRANSITIONING THE CHURCH

Almost all the steps in transitioning outlined so far have to do with leadership. It takes plenty of time and effort to bring the power people to a place where new ideas can be tried. Only then can the leadership team introduce the cell church concept to the wider church.

A congregation of perhaps 100 or fewer could probably make the transition as a whole church. But another idea, appropriate for larger churches, is to transition ministry by ministry. The Taipei Ling Leung Church in Taiwan, pastored by Rev. Chow Shen Chu, took this approach. With a congregation of some 4,000 people, they have been more successful than any other church in that region in transitioning to the cell structure.

The Taipei church had dozens of departments and ministries. I think they had seven separate fellowships for young adults alone! The leadership team began looking at the various departments and chose one that seemed most open to trying the cell model. The church leaders then began training the leaders of this department in the same way the core leadership was trained. They met together, worked with them, and prepared them as cell leaders. During transition, they decided the department's small groups would designate one meeting per month as a cell meeting, with the rest as regular fellowship meetings or Bible studies. Soon the cell meetings increased to two, three, and four times per month. After a while, the whole department became a cell ministry. In this way, department by department, the entire church turned around.

Here is an outline of some common steps, whether transitioning a whole church or a department or ministry within a church:

1. Work with the leadership to plan the master calendar for the year.

2. Plan a leaders' retreat and share the cell concept with the leadership of the department (or church).

3. Begin cell leader training with the department's (or church's) current leaders.

4. Begin zone supervisor training.

5. Share the vision with the whole department (or church), once the leaders are prepared.

6. Launch the cell ministry. Declare that as of this date, this department (or church) is a cell department (or church). Even

with the full structure not yet in place, a public statement will let everyone know that this is the direction to which the department (or church) has committed.

Some pastors of large, traditional, program-based churches may find the prospect of transitioning their church, even on a gradual ministry-by-ministry basis, too overwhelming. In some cases, the most effective approach might be to launch cell church plants in the same city or region. If the Lord has captured your heart with the cell vision, but turning your church around seems tougher than turning a battleship, do not despair. Gather leaders who share your vision and equip them to birth a new church in the cell model. The new church plant, using a pure cell genetic code without the old DNA of the traditional church, should be able to grow more quickly and reach segments of your community that remain untouched by the gospel.

AVOIDING PITFALLS

I have observed some common pitfalls among pastors and churches who desire to make the transition to a cell church. Let me mention four to avoid:

1. *Not realizing how much time is required.* Transition takes significant time. Allow people to ask questions and raise objections without judging them or getting discouraged. Spend enough time sharing the vision and pressing forward so that, even if you hit a stone wall, you will feel assured that you have acted as a responsible leader no matter whether you are led to resignation or revolution.

2. *Not having past experiences to draw from.* Not long ago, churches had little choice about this situation. These days, more and more churches have gone through transition or are in different stages. Pastors in the same city who are pursuing the cell model can

avoid pitfalls by coming together regularly to talk, exchange ideas, and pray for one another. In the midst of such a major structural change and paradigm shift, leaders need encouragement and hope from others who understand the process.

3. *Using solutions from the old paradigm.* This is a common problem I have discussed previously. In the face of obstacles, turning to solutions that worked within the prior structure seems natural. But fatal dangers lurk down this path. Be careful not to water down the pure cell church structure as your goal.

4. *Getting caught up in forms and losing sight of principles.* Review the cell church principles periodically to keep them in the front of your mind at all times. Before taking a step or implementing a program, stop to ask how this step lines up with one or more principles of the cell church. Otherwise, you might begin to steer away from the cell model without even realizing it.

AVAILABLE HELP AND RESOURCES

I will close this chapter by mentioning different levels of help available from Faith Community Baptist Church. Many of these have been mentioned in previous chapters.

• Every spring we host the International Conference on Cell Group Churches.

• The TESS Intensive Course on the Cell Church is a follow-up training program for senior pastors and key pastors, offered each September for about two and a half weeks.

• The 18-month TESS Training School raises up zone pastors through a combination of classwork and practical training. The

12-month classroom part of the program is divided into modules of three or four months each so that pastors who cannot attend the full program all at once may register for each of three parts separately. The first of the modules consists of the "core essentials" and is a prerequisite for the other two parts, although students may complete Part One without continuing with the others. Support courses focus on such areas as counseling, leadership, coaching skills, and so on.

- Our school also offers a three-month series of courses with training in theology, the Bible, and so forth. This series benefits pastors or leaders who do not have a seminary or Bible school background.

- FCBC provides internship opportunities. Participants serve in a district and get hands-on experience with the cell church. Student visas are available for lengthy stays in Singapore.

- Beyond Singapore, the Lord sometimes calls us to minister in other countries by spreading the vision for the cell church. I and my team are most likely to come when I can see that a mature, existing group will be able to carry on the process of transition and equipping. Then all we need to do is rally the key leaders.

- Then occasionally the Lord will put a particular region on our hearts and tell us to go deep. In these situations we bring churches together to teach them, start a zone pastor training school, and expend considerable resources in personnel and finances. My pastoral team and I go to Taiwan, for instance, four or five times per year, for a few days each trip. We have also committed to in-depth training in Kazakhstan. We can provide this level of help only when the churches in that region are ready, with a few working examples of the cell model already in place.

Faith Community Baptist Church has plenty of history with what works and what doesn't work when transitioning to the cell church. We have made mistakes, learned from them, and continue to do both. By now we have systematized most of our training and equipping resources. But we are by no means the only source of help available to churches wanting assistance in transitioning to the cell structure. Thank God for growing numbers of resources, opportunities, and diverse models from which everyone, including FCBC, can learn. As we teach and encourage one another, the Holy Spirit continues to anoint and empower the cell church movement as it spreads city by city, nation by nation, around the globe.

Eleven

REPOSSESSING THE CITY:

— It is Time for War! —

I always knew that if I could not become a pastor I would become a soldier. Military strategy and tactics have fascinated me since my childhood days. Maybe that's why my favorite Old Testament book is Joshua. I love to read about the Israelite army conquering the land with the power of God.

But from my country's birth until now, the Singaporean army has never seen combat. This situation did not attract me to the army's ranks! A military career without opportunity to challenge a real enemy in battle would have seemed like spending my life training as the understudy for an actor who never got sick.

In a sense, however, I have become both a pastor and a soldier. The Bible describes the people of God as engaged in real-life combat with an enemy determined to destroy us. Unlike the Singaporean army, the army of God doesn't just play war games in peacetime. While our conflict takes place in spiritual rather than physical realms, the danger is just as real—and the stakes are higher.

Some Christians do not like warfare imagery or terminology. Certainly the Bible uses a variety of analogies for our roles as believers, and not everyone will find them equally appealing. But, like it or not, Scripture calls us to take our stand and fight as armed warriors against the spiritual rulers of darkness (see, for instance, Psalm 144:1, Psalm 149:6, 2 Corinthians 10:3-4, 1 Timothy 6:12, and 2 Timothy 2:3). We contend not against people, as Ephesians 6:12 says, but against the devil, his demons, and their evil activity. Our enemy aims to capture as many people as possible, both eternally and here on earth, and keep them from glorifying their Creator. We fight Satan best, then, by welcoming King Jesus into our hearts, our cities, our nations. Loving and exalting Jesus, while we love and bless others in His name, will defeat the devil and his schemes.

From the first day of my ministry, even when pastoring a small church in Dallas while I attended seminary, I have cried out in echo of Revelation 11:15, "Lord, I want to see the day when the kingdom of this world will become the kingdom of our Lord Jesus Christ!" I want to rejoice as more and more lives and communities, held captive by the enemy for too long, get reclaimed for Christ, their rightful owner.

Yes, it is time for war! Since Christ's death and resurrection, however, we already have the guarantee of victory. If there is one verse that could paint the journey I have experienced with God in both my ministry and my personal walk with Him, it would be 2 Corinthians 2:14: "But thanks be to God, who always leads us in triumphal procession in Christ and through us spreads everywhere the fragrance of the knowledge of him."

This key verse, which has undergirded my life and ministry, refers to the way a triumphant Roman general returned with the spoils of battle to be presented to the emperor and the people. I want to be part of the spiritual army that captures territory for God and delivers as many people as possible out of the dominion of darkness and into the kingdom of light.

We are an army at war. I believe that the power of God manifests most clearly not in the church buildings where we sing our praises to Him but rather on the streets where the people are. God loves and is partial toward sinners. So if we want to see God in action, we must go out and serve the poor and the sick and broken. In so doing we will declare war against the devil, and will see God arise and call forth His army to repossess cities and nations.

Four truths stand out about this wartime we now live in: (1) It is God's time. (2) It is breakthrough time. (3) It is our time. (4) It is victory time.

It is God's Time

As I look back on the last decade, I marvel at everything God has been doing, both globally and in my own region and nation. At the beginning of chapter 2, I summarized a few major world movements in the church today. The Holy Spirit, for instance, is renewing and anointing His church in signs and wonders never seen before. The move of God in world evangelization has produced fresh strategies to reach all people groups. The Lord is reviving prayer in many forms—powerful, united prayer that first purges us of sin and then invades and recaptures enemy territory. And He is preparing new wineskins such as the cell church to receive the Spirit's outpouring. All of the movements of God equip and enable us to repossess our cities for His kingdom.

In Singapore, I see astonishing change in just the last few years, especially since October 1993 when I attended the Gideon's Army meeting of the International Spiritual Warfare Network in Seoul, Korea. In the years since then, the unity of pastors in Singapore has spread like wildfire. Other global observers say it is unprecedented. The key lies in the relationships of love and honest accountability that have developed, not just unity around a task or an event. Pastors meet together and take offerings for each other. They support and cheer for one another, and rejoice when they see God's grace manifested in others' lives. And with increased unity, increased anointing flows.

Not only pastors but lay church members reflect this move of the Spirit. People in the same neighborhood come together spontaneously and pray for one another, cry with one another, and reach out to others in unity. United prayer is taking place in public as well as in private. These things do not mean that we are better or holier or seeking God more than previous generations. All significant movements occur only in the power of the Spirit. It is simply God's work and God's time.

Of the approximately 400 Christian churches in Singapore, more than 100 are committed to the vision of Love Singapore (described in chapter 4), with at least 120 involved in one way or another. Because these include some of the country's largest churches, more than one-third of the Christians in this nation have now united to see Singapore reached for Jesus.

The climate of our city-state is changing. We have reports that non-Christians approach believers to ask, "What must I do to be saved?" We have established a spiritual beachhead for the army of the Lord and believe that, from there, the Holy Spirit will enable us to launch more drives to liberate territory now held by the evil one.

God on the Move Around the World

My friend Ed Silvoso often says, "In the city, there is only one church and many congregations." I now have a bigger dream for which I am believing. I want to see in the whole continent of Asia only one church, united under Jesus Christ. I want to see Christians come together and say, for instance, "Let's go as one body and love Indonesia. Let's operate as one church in one name—not the name of a denomination or a congregation, but the name of Jesus Christ, whose name is above every name." When we work together this way, we will experience firsthand how this region will be saved as one church and many congregations.

I see this kind of anointing at work in South Africa, in Brazil, in Argentina, in the United States. God is going to piece us together like an exquisite mosaic. Everyone will fit in as we join our hands in prayer. In this way we will take the world for Jesus. We will rise up as one church in the name of Christ.

Do you know that God has told us exactly when Jesus is coming back? First Thessalonians 5:2 says the day of the Lord will come like a thief in the night—but only for those in darkness. Verses 4–6 go on to declare that the children of light should not be surprised by this event. According to Matthew 24:14, Jesus will return when the body of Christ rises as one beautiful bride and joins hands across the earth to see all the nations of the world reached with the gospel. The Lord will come when the bride is ready, and we are His bride.

I believe we live in an era when the wineskin of God's glory is being changed. God is pouring out a new wine and creating a new church to receive it. Our Commander-in-Chief will see victory over the enemy, using an anointed church He has raised up as a mighty invading army. We are now moving into an apostolic age when God is appointing generals over His troops. These leaders hold recognized authority and anointing. They can stand up and say "The time is now!" Then everyone responds, "Yes!" and forges ahead to possess the land.

"But thanks be to God...." Truly, every day I wake up and thank God that I live in this era. It is God's time.

IT IS BREAKTHROUGH TIME

It is also time for breakthroughs. God is telling us that as we declare war, we are going to see the victory of the Lord, and the fragrance of the knowledge of Him will spread everywhere. Some people will reject it; others will accept it. But that Word will go forth to every community as a powerful work of God. In fact, during the year 1999, the church of Jesus Christ in Singapore has committed to pray for every man, woman, and child by name in this nation.

We are seeing breakthroughs in the body of Christ. We are mapping strongholds, asking God where our "Jerichos" are, and prayerwalking each neighborhood until we plant a cell that takes hold and grows. The church in Singapore has become a light of God's love to the nation. Even *The Straits Times*, our major English-language newspaper, covered the inauguration of the Love Singapore Fund on page 3. The flow of abundant resources has enabled the church to redistribute wealth to the poor.

We expect a major breakthrough at Faith Community Baptist Church, too. Years ago God gave us a vision that by the end of the year 2000 He wanted us to have 5,000 cells. At our annual planning meeting toward the end of 1998 we did a survey and found that we had 620 cells—after ten years as a cell church.

I struggled with the implications of this number, because God has given me a vision for all of Singapore. I kept asking the Lord for a strategy on how to win this sector or that neighborhood. But God told me, "It is not for you to know. I have given you the vision for the whole land, but you are to release others to whom I will give the strategy for reaching each neighborhood."

I went back to my pastoral team, laid the vision before them again, and empowered them to change it. Because I cannot generate 5,000 cells myself, the whole team needs to own the vision by faith in order for the Holy Spirit to move mightily to accomplish it. I told each district pastor to seek the Lord and ask, "How many cells can I believe God for?" After a week of prayer, we came back together and added the figures. We determined that we could believe God for a total of 2,000 FCBC cells by the end of the year 2000. Yet we had received a vision for 5,000 cells. Had we heard God wrongly?

Fresh Vision Arises

Just then, the Lord led me to a book about the explosive growth of cells in Bogotá, Colombia. The author spotlighted the International Charismatic Mission, pastored by César Castellanos. In 1996 this church established a goal to grow to 10,000 cells by the end of the year. But by October they had just 5,600 cells. The author confessed that he had made a sarcastic remark at that time: "One characteristic of this church is they do not change their goals to conform to reality." Later, however, he had to repent, because by December 1996 the church not only met their goal but exceeded 10,000 cells by 600! Moreover, in 1997 the church purposed to triple their home cell groups, and successfully reached 30,000 cells.

"We do not change our goals to conform to reality." This statement spoke to me. As I mulled it over, God said, "You are to follow a greater reality, the reality of the realm of the Spirit."

I went back to my pastoral team and we committed to asking God if we had heard correctly about the 5,000 cells. After prayer, each one confirmed this. We then went back to the Lord for the strategy to accomplish His will.

He told us to double every cell by the end of 1999, for a total of about 1,300 cells. This first step was a challenging goal in itself, because the fact of the matter is that FCBC does not always fulfill its vision of multiplying each cell within 12 to 18 months. At one time a survey showed that ten percent of our cells had never multiplied in three years! Yet we remain committed to the vision, and each pastor had faith to believe each cell could double by the end of 1999.

The next step of the strategy God gave us was to establish four cell-planting efforts within each cell by December 2000, so each of the approximately 1,300 groups would quadruple by the end of that year. As we pray for one another, we believe God will perfect the spiritual skill and technology of planting cells in every school, office, club, housing complex, and sector of society. We also believe God will increase our burden for the lost and our heart-cry to see every group reached for Christ.

Accomplishing FCBC's goal of 5,000 cells will by no means complete the task of evangelism in Singapore. For one thing, the country has about 10,000 "blocks," or high-rise buildings, of government-subsidized apartment flats, and each needs a cell. As we do the work to which God has called us, others will be inspired to do their part. The whole body of Christ, joined together in the power of God, will see this land saturated with the fragrance of the knowledge of Him. It is time for breakthroughs.

It is Our Time

This wartime is not only God's time; it is also our time. Let's take another look at 2 Corinthians 2:14: "But thanks be to God, who always leads *us* in triumphal procession in Christ and through *us* spreads everywhere the fragrance of the knowledge of him" (emphasis added). Think about the implications. We believe that God can take the land, of course. But do we really believe that *we* can take the land, that God can do it through *us?*

The Lord is stirring faith that we, His people, are called and empowered to accomplish God's will on this earth. It is time to rise and declare with authority that we have been sent by God for a purpose. If it's going to be done, it's going to be done through us.

During seminary I learned about the theology of dispensationalism. I believe that the most damaging aspect of this theology—beyond its denial of supernatural gifts—is its tendency to make Christians passive. According to much of pre-tribulation thinking, the church gamely carries on while the world goes downhill. Then, just before the worst happens, the church gets snatched out of the scene. What an anemic picture of our impact on society! For my part, I believe I'm going to live through the tribulation. That should be the most exciting time in human history, and I don't want to miss it! I want to be around when God shakes the heavens and the earth.

In these days the Lord is restoring to the church the five-fold ministry of Ephesians 4:11–13: "It was he who gave some to be apostles, some to be prophets, some to be evangelists, and some to be pastors and teachers, to prepare God's people for works of service, so that the body of Christ may be built up until we all reach unity in the faith and in the knowledge of the Son of God and become mature, attaining to the whole measure of the fullness of Christ." In this passage I see increasing measures of growth and equipping promised to the body. I don't think the church of Jesus Christ has risen to its full stature yet, but the Word says it will. This is our time to become more perfected and victorious as the power of God works in us.

As the church ascends in maturity, we play a key role in releasing the Holy Spirit's power for breakthroughs. The kingdom of God will come because we bring it back. I love what pastor and author Jack Hayford says in his book *Prayer is Invading the Impossible*: "Without God, we cannot. Without us, He will not."

Dominion over Our Land

The Bible indicates that we as human beings have authority over territory. Psalm 115:16 says, "The highest heavens belong to the LORD, but the earth he has given to man." For this reason, when Jesus Christ came to redeem us, He had to become man. God has power to repossess the earth, but He gave to humankind the authority to do so. This is our realm. The Lord didn't commission us to win Mars for Christ or to win some galaxy for Christ, but He gave us the earth. The Second Adam restored to us the blessing of the first Adam—to possess this land and to have dominion over it. The earth is ours, and we each have authority and responsibility to claim the portion where we live.

Deuteronomy 32ß:8 says, "When the Most High gave the nations their inheritance, when he divided all mankind, he set up boundaries for the peoples according to the number of the sons of Israel." Acts 17:26 echoes this theme: "From one man he made every nation of men, that they should inhabit the whole earth; and he determined the times set for them and the exact places where they should live." When God planned the earth, He set the boundaries where people should live. It was no accident where each of us was born or where we are living. The place God assigned to us is where we have our inheritance.

From Ezekiel 47:21–23 we learn that even the migrants who came and settled in the land received an inheritance from God, just like the native-born. Our birth place and our dwelling place are the exact locations God has given to each of us, and we have a right to that land.

The government of Singapore carries deep concern over the "brain drain," as many skilled and educated people from our country leave for greener pastures. Because of the truth revealed in scriptures such as these, I always tell Singaporeans, "God forbid that you should emigrate—unless God tells you to. The heritage of this land belongs to you. Christians, more than anyone, should love Singapore. When God birthed us and caused us to live here, He had a divine purpose. And as long as we stay in this land, we are going to possess the spiritual inheritance not only of this land but also of the nations."

The more we commit to a territory, the more authority we can wield in it. Each of us has the right to speak over our neighborhood, our city, or our nation, and tell the devil, "This land belongs to me! My Father gave it to me, and I serve you with eviction orders!" This is not simply a triumphalist attitude—it is the Word of God.

IT IS VICTORY TIME

Our theme verse in 2 Corinthians 2:14 reads, "But thanks be to God, who always"—not sometimes, but *always*—"leads us in triumphal procession in Christ and through us spreads everywhere the fragrance of the knowledge of him." Even though we might experience setbacks, ultimate victory is promised—always. With this verse undergirding my life and ministry, I remain incurably and unapologetically optimistic. I don't expect to lose. I've read the last page of the Bible. It says we win, and I take it literally. Tough times and challenges provide precisely the kind of situation when God acts in the most exciting ways.

We have a role in working out this victory. For instance, the door to Indonesia stands wide open now. Indonesia is going to see the salvation of the Lord, because God is shaking it and the people of God have a right to possess the land. One of my professors at Dallas Theological Seminary, Dr. Howard Hendricks, once quoted an army sergeant as saying to his troops, "Men, we are surrounded by enemies—and don't you dare let any one of them escape."

Some of us will die for Jesus in this wartime. But God will still have the victory, whether our contribution to the war effort comes through martyrdom or aggressive assaults on enemy territory. Fear, resignation, or passive waiting for our heavenly home will not speed victory nor help rescue souls in bondage to the devil. General George S. Patton, Jr., colorful commander of U.S. forces during World War II, once gave advice to some of his soldiers. In sanitized paraphrase, he told them, "The object of war is not to die for your country, but to make the other guy die for his."

Every time I take a spiritual hit or fall, I declare, "God, the victory is around the corner; it's coming." I never deny the reality of the situation, but I recognize a higher reality in God's Word and promises. Pastors need to pray against a spirit of defeat. God will impart leadership authority as pastors stand up in faith to overcome the dominion of darkness. People who see the glory of God in their leader's eyes will march on in solidarity.

Any time you make changes or go through transitions, you will experience setbacks. Even though victory is assured, problems may crop up in at least three areas, so leaders do well to watch out for these:

Problems in Relationships

When transitioning or making changes, you must maintain intimate communication with the Lord in order to proceed in His divine wisdom. He will give you words to share and faith to release in others. But even with careful planning, relationships will be tested. Every time I see a change coming in my own ministry, relationships come into question. Sometimes these kinds of issues arise because of demonic influence, but other times the Lord is at work, often trying to reassign people. Faith Community Baptist Church, remember, was born out of a split, the most difficult time in my life.

In the first chapter I told that story—the pain and confusion I experienced before I was fired, and the Lord's clear word to me out of John 16:21 that He was bringing forth a "new baby" that would launch me into a new ministry. During the last two years I have experienced a season no less painful than when I was thrown out of my own church. The hurt and difficulties in relationships cut just as deeply. But again I hear God saying to me, "I am birthing something in your life and you are going through labor pain. I'm giving you a new ministry. You must press on and claim My victory."

A Period of Inefficiency

To make it through a transition so your church can grow and reach more of the lost, the church may need to stagnate for a time or even regress slightly in size. Transition costs resources that have to get plowed into the change process before progress can come.

The effort is like changing gears in a manual transmission car. Every time you want to shift to a higher gear, you first have to disengage the gear you are in. When God wants to make a change and engage you on a higher level, you will often find the situation scary or confusing for a while, because things don't seem to work the way they used to. You may experience a sense of restlessness or lack of control. Because the strategies of the cell church are new to you, the road of transition can get messy. But God says, "It's OK. I'm disengaging something so that I may engage you on a different level, on a path to victory." He will always lead us in triumph.

Emotional Fatigue

The drain of transition and change takes a toll on our human bodies and souls. A few years ago I felt so tired I seriously considered retirement. The Lord revealed to me that I was experiencing emotional fatigue. Many pastors face the scourge of burnout, especially during difficult and challenging seasons, such as transitions.

God gave me fresh courage through His Word. Isaiah 40:31 says that those who wait upon the Lord will renew their strength. During that year I contemplated retiring, the Lord led me to undertake a 40-day fast. I had never fasted previously for longer than a week. For those 40 days I took no solid food, only water and some juices. I came to work every day; I even played polo. And at the end of that season of waiting on Him, God gave me a breakthrough. I came through knowing the renewal of the Lord in my life.

THE TIME IS NOW

My prayer for the readers of this book is that God will strengthen and renew you to rise and take your place in the service of our Commander-in-Chief. I believe He is training each of us to be warriors, sergeants, captains, or even generals in His army. While the war rages around us in the heavenly realms, God will give us new vision and strategies: new vision to see with eyes of compassion the many lost souls held captive by the enemy, and new strategies to reclaim them for the Lord in unprecedented numbers.

With our hearts fixed on God's promises from His Word, we can lay hold of the victory He has ordained and move forward in courage and faith to advance His kingdom. Let the church arise—God deserves it. The time is now!

— *Index* —

10/40 Window, 59–60, 156

C

D

Dallas, Texas, 202

Dallas Theological Seminary, 52, 84, 92, 211

David, king, 109

da Vinci, Leonardo, 161

Dawn International Network, 10

DAWN Report, 10

Day to Change the World, global, 77

deliverance, 48, 78, 84, 92, 98, 130, 156, 202. *See also* demons; spiritual warfare

demons, 48, 83–84, 92, 95, 98, 103, 130, 156, 202, 212. *See also* deliverance; strongholds

discipleship, 11, 40, 61, 74, 76, 157, 162, 167, 169, 171. *See also* equipping; mobilization

dispensationalism, 208

district pastors, 39, 41, 49, 55, 56–57, 104, 153, 206

districts, 39–41, 155, 198. *See also* congregations

Divine Conquest, The, 85–86

E

East Asia, 59

East, Eastern, Easterners, 38

edification, 46–47, 65, 66, 95. *See also* discipleship; pastoral care

Egypt, 24, 27, 87

Elijah, 29, 109, 181

equipping, 13, 31, 32, 57–58, 74, 145, 162–73, 182–83, 190, 191, 198, 209; for evangelism, 118, 127–32, 136–37, 155, 168–70; within the cell, 11–12, 37, 53, 56, 153, 166–67. *See also* discipleship; leadership training; mobilization

Erdenet, Mongolia, 43–44

Evangelical Dictionary of Theology, 125

evangelism, 11–12, 34, 51, 65, 66–67, 76, 78, 94–96, 99, 109, 117–42, 165, 181, 182, 207; as a lifestyle, 54, 127–28, 133, 168; cell growth through, 35, 37–38, 46–47, 118, 138–40. *See also* body evangelism; cell planting; cycles of harvest; harvest events; oikos evangelism; outreach; missions; servant evangelism; type "A" evangelism; type "B" evangelism

F

Faith Community Baptist Church (FCBC): birth of, 19, 20–21, 113, 177, 212; growth factors at, 24, 28, 34, 110; strategy of, 33, 70, 73, 75–76, 147, 207; transitioning process of, 175–76, 177–83; vision of, 33, 40, 41, 69–70, 73–75, 80, 146–47, 150–51, 155–56, 177, 179–80, 206–8. *See also* church growth: in FCBC

Family Journeys Together, The, 171

First Baptist Church of Modesto, California, 71, 113

five-fold ministries, 31, 109, 208

"Four Spiritual Laws," 51, 62

sponsors, 53, 57, 166–69
Straits Times, The, 206
strategy. *See* FCBC: strategy of; unity: of strategy
strongholds, 129–30, 131–32, 153, 166, 167, 205. *See also* demons; spiritual warfare
Sweden, Swedes, 43

T

Taipei Ling Liang Church, 194–95
Taipei, Taiwan, 194–95
Taiwan, 194, 198
"Taking the City Walk," 80
Taoists, 124
TESS Intensive, 172, 197. *See also* T͟O͟U͟C͟H Equipping Station System (TESS)
TESS Training School, 172, 197–98. *See also* T͟O͟U͟C͟H Equipping Station System (TESS)
Texas, 202
"Thank God It's Friday" (T.G.I.F.), 135, 146
That None Should Perish, 77
Time magazine, 17–18
tongues, heavenly, 19–20, 23, 92, 93, 94–96, 129. *See also* Holy Spirit: gifts of
T͟O͟U͟C͟H Community Services (TCS), 78–79, 81, 140–41, 152
T͟O͟U͟C͟H Equipping Station System (TESS), 57, 170–72
T͟O͟U͟C͟H Ministries International (TMI), 81
touch points, 133, 140–41. *See also* service to the community
Tozer, A. W., 85
traditional church, 36, 37, 44, 45, 58, 71, 81, 93, 107, 162–63, 187. *See also* program-based church
transformation (of communities), 10, 13, 70, 77, 81, 204
transitioning to the cell church, 13, 42, 46, 49, 57, 74, 81, 97, 117–18, 138, 156, 162–63, 168, 175–99, 212; prerequisites for, 31–35, 69, 86, 107; within leadership, 183–94; within wider church, 194–96. *See also* FCBC: transitioning process of
type "A" evangelism, 127, 128–29, 135, 136, 154, 169
type "A" unbelievers, 120, 128, 137–38, 140
type "B" evangelism, 127, 130–32, 138, 144–45, 148, 154
type "B" unbelievers, 120, 128, 166

U

Ulaanbaatar, Mongolia, 43
United Prayer Track, 77
United States, 17–18, 19, 81, 92, 161, 204, 211. *See also* California, Colorado, Maryland, Texas
unity, 76–80, 186, 203–5, 209; in prayer, 30, 203–4; of strategy, 71–73, 155; of vision, 32–33, 42, 69, 111–12, 152, 187

V

value change, 51, 53, 163–64
Vineyard Christian Fellowship, 97
vision. *See* cell church: vision of; FCBC: vision of; unity: of vision
Vision 2001. *See* Love Singapore

W

Wagner, C. Peter, 76–77, 131, 187
Wagner Leadership Institute, 172
Welcome stage of cell agenda, 47. *See also* "Four W's"
West Africa, 59
West, Western, Westerners, 38, 61, 62–63, 66
Wimber, John, 97, 129
wineskins, fresh/new, 10–13, 28, 31, 46, 49, 187–88, 203, 205.
Word stage of cell agenda, 48–49, 54, 168. *See also* "Four W's"
Works stage of cell agenda, 48, 127, 136–37, 148. *See also* "Four W's"
WorldCells International (WCI), 81, 156
world evangelization, 12–13, 21, 30–31, 38, 72, 115, 172, 203, 205. *See also* 10/40
    Window; missions; outreach
World Prayer Center, 76
worship (praise), 11, 40, 78, 79–80, 148, 176–77, 178, 191, 202
Worship stage of cell agenda, 47–48, 65, 126. *See also* "Four W's"

Y

Yaegar, Bill, 71, 113–14, 115
Year of Equipping, 128, 156, 164–70, 192
Year of Mobilization, 156
Your New Journey Guide, 167

Z

zone pastors, 39, 41, 55, 56–59, 104, 153, 171, 172, 181, 191, 193, 197–98
zones, 155, 191
zone supervisors, 39, 41, 55, 56–60, 104, 156, 166, 171, 181–82, 191, 193, 195